Strengthen Yourself in the LORD

HOW TO RELEASE
THE HIDDEN POWER
OF GOD IN YOUR LIFE

by

BILL JOHNSON

 All emphasis within Scripture quotations is the author's own. Please note that Destiny Image's publishing style capitalizes certain pronouns in Scripture that refer to the Father, Son, and Holy Spirit, and may differ from some publishers' styles. Take note that the name satan and related names are not capitalized. We choose not to acknowledge him, even to the point of violating grammatical rules.

DESTINY IMAGE® PUBLISHERS, INC.
P.O. Box 310, Shippensburg, PA 17257-0310

"*Speaking to the Purposes of God for this Generation and for the Generations to Come.*"

This book and all other Destiny Image, Revival Press, Mercy Place, Fresh Bread, Destiny Image Fiction, and Treasure House books are available at Christian bookstores and distributors worldwide.

For a U.S. bookstore nearest you, call 1-800-722-6774.

For more information on foreign distributors, call 717-532-3040.

Or reach us on the Internet: www.destinyimage.com

ISBN 10: 0-7684-2427-5
ISBN 13: 978-0-7684-2427-0

For Worldwide Distribution, Printed in the U.S.A.

3 4 5 6 7 8 9 10 11 / 09 08 07

DEDICATION

I dedicate this book to Randy Clark: Your humility, integrity, and passion for God has affected millions of people—and I am one. Your encouragement and support has been monumental in my life. Thank you for your friendship and for the example you have been to me in stewarding the life of miracles. Thanks, Randy.

ACKNOWLEDGEMENTS

Thanks to Dann Farrelly and Pam Spinosi for your editorial help, again. Thanks to Mary Walker and Judy Franklin for your constant encouragement and help in putting this book together. Special thanks to Allison Armerding for helping me with the actual writing of this book. You are all priceless!

Endorsements

In many decades of ministry across the world, I have discovered that people, whatever their background, have two primary questions: "Who am I?" and "What is my purpose?" Bill Johnson masterfully answers these questions as he shares the tools that the Lord has taught him to use to strengthen himself. This great pastor's insights will show you how God has equipped you with all the tools necessary to fulfill your destiny. Whatever dire circumstances you have gone through, this book will help you lay hold of God's provision to finish the journey in victory as you "strengthen yourself in the Lord."

Dr. Mahesh Chavda
Author, *The Hidden Power of Prayer and Fasting*

In the midst of a world of chaos and confusion in the atmosphere around us, the enemy attempts to develop a plan to take advantage of us. One key to our lives is not allowing seeming defeats, discouragements, and robbing strategies of the enemy to overtake us and create a failure mentality in our thought process. In *Strengthen Yourself in the Lord: How to Release the Hidden Power of God in Your Life,* Bill Johnson has created a way of thinking to help you develop a victory plan for your life. This book will cause you to develop a mentality of blessing, being blessed, celebration, and praise that will unlock the BEST that the Lord has for you in the future!

Dr. Chuck D. Pierce
President, Glory of Zion International, Inc.
Vice President, Global Harvest Ministries

Bill's new book provides rich, powerful encouragement for every Christian fighting for spiritual survival, and that would include most of us at some point. But more than that, Bill points the way forward for all of us who want to press on toward our high calling in Jesus, not allowing anything to hold us back from our destiny. Bill speaks from experience, and his life, relationships and the testimonies that follow his ministry are evidence that he knows the way...

Rolland and Heidi Baker
Iris Ministries

Bill Johnson's "toolbag" is loaded with the necessary equipment to build a life of faith and blessing. I was assured that no ministry that walks in the measure of revelation that Bill does is accidental, and once again, I see the practical ways that the Father has sustained him and advanced him in a most remarkable and gifted ministry. I believe it is the basis for who he is and what he does.

Bishop Joseph L. Garlington

Contents

INTRODUCTION

It's time to be strong and of great courage. I don't know that there has ever been a time when courage and faith were more needed. But I don't say this because of the darkness of the hour. That is a given. I say it because of the realm of God's promises that linger over the Church, waiting for someone to see it—to believe it—to say yes to what could be!

To live in courage requires encouragement. And sometimes the only one to encourage you is you. Not knowing how to strengthen ourselves has cost the Church dearly. It is the key to promotion! It is what turned David's darkest hour into the *backdoor* to the throne room. And it will be the same for you. When you learn how to strengthen yourself, you will reach your destiny, fulfill your God-born dreams, and become a person who can accurately represent Jesus—re-presenting Jesus to the world.

Chapter 1

The Secret to David's Promotion

If you want to kill giants,

follow a giant killer!

King David towers above all other Old Testament figures in this sense—he is remembered not so much for the greatness of his actions, but for the greatness of his heart for God. His passionate heart set him apart in God's eyes long before he ever won great military victories, before he revolutionized the nature of worship in Israel, or even ushered in Israel's Golden Age of economic and spiritual prosperity. While David was still in obscurity, God saw that he was a man after His own heart. (See Acts 13:22.)

What was the evidence of David's heart after God? Scripture indicates two primary aspects of David's life before he was anointed king. First, when nobody was looking, when nobody was calling prayer meetings or leading a revival in Judah, David was pouring out his heart in worship and prayer to God in the fields where he tended his father's sheep. With no one around, his pursuit of God was motivated by nothing but a desire to know God for His own sake.

David's relationship with the Lord was highly unusual for his day because the entire paradigm for worship in Israel at the time was focused on the sacrifice of animals to temporarily deal with sin, and not the sacrifice of praise from the heart. His heart led him beyond the letter of the law to the heart of the Lord, Himself. Secondly, David's battles against the lion and the bear revealed his heart for God because he relied completely on God for victory. This trust indicated that David's heart for the Lord was not something that changed according to his circumstances. He had integrity of heart. (See 1 Sam. 17:37.)

Groomed to Reign

God did not bring the *man after His heart* straight from the pasture to the palace. Incredibly, David did not assume the throne until 10-13 years *after* Samuel had anointed him to be king. In those interim years, David endured more difficulty, persecution, and rejection than many of us face in a lifetime. He probably didn't expect it to take so long to become king.

In contrast, Saul, the previous king, had no such difficulty; he was crowned very shortly after being anointed by Samuel. But God did not want another King Saul. While Saul was truly the best man Israel had to offer when they demanded a king (see 1 Sam. 8:6), his heart had not been groomed through testing before he assumed the throne. As king, Saul was entrusted with a measure of anointing to lead the armies of Israel to victory and shepherd the people. Yet, without the strength of character that only comes by winning private battles, these public victories exposed the previously hidden weakness of Saul's heart toward God. That weakness, combined with his growing appetite for the favor of man, led him to bring glory to himself and disobey the Lord. Saul's untested heart allowed that which was given to make him successful, to ultimately destroy him.

So David, even though he already possessed a heart for the Lord, was led into years of testing that groomed him to handle the glory and responsibility of the throne. The scriptural account of this season in David's life is filled with lessons on the kinds of character tests we all face on the road to fulfilling our destiny in God. But the real question—what is it about David that ultimately qualifies him to become king? What brings about the moment in which God says, "OK, now you're ready"? I would like to suggest that it was David's ability to do something in the face of the deepest betrayal and rejection imaginable. When he stood completely alone, that is when David "*strengthened himself in the Lord his God*" (1 Sam. 30:6).

THE ROLE OF REJECTION

Seeing the progression in the tests David faced is valuable for understanding the significance of this choice that became the tipping point for his being enthroned as king. The following is a "*Reader's Digest*" version of David's life in the years after he was anointed.

These years actually began with apparent success. David's unique intimacy with the Lord had already set him apart and given him what no other man in Israel had—great courage, fueled by a righteous indignation at the enemies who were taunting the armies of the living God. David, armor-less and alone, boldly defied the odds and ran at Goliath, winning a great victory over the giant as well as the Philistines. This exploit instantly earned him favor with the people and King Saul. As a result, He moved into the palace, became best friends with the king's son, and married the king's daughter. By all accounts, the fulfillment of Samuel's word over him seemed imminent.

But then King Saul got wind of a song that the women of the city were singing, "Saul has killed his thousands, and David his ten thousands." Consumed with jealousy, he launched a campaign to end David's life. After dodging Saul's spears, David painfully came to terms with the reality that he was going to have to leave Jerusalem to survive. He probably had no idea that this demonized madman would chase him for over a decade as far away from the throne as possible. Saul's rejection of him was the first sign that David's schooling for the kingship was based on testing his ability to believe and walk in the Word over his life, even when the circumstances seemed to completely oppose and deny his destiny.

We can see another character test he faced when, after leaving Jerusalem and hiding in several places for a while, David rescued the village of Keilah from the Philistines. He found out that Saul knew he was there, so he asked the Lord whether he would come after him, and whether the citizens he had just saved—his own Jewish brothers—were going to protect him or turn him over to Saul. God said, "He's coming for you, and they're going to turn you over." Rejected again, he headed for the wilderness.

By this time he also had some followers, but they were "*everyone who was in distress, everyone who was in debt, and everyone who was discontented...*" (1 Sam. 22:2). They were the rejects of society. David demonstrated a true king's heart by embracing these men, and spent the next ten years or so training them in life and in warfare. Under his leadership, these "rejects" became his "mighty men." (Interestingly, at least four of these men ended up killing giants, just as David had done. If you want to kill giants, follow a giant killer!) Eventually David moved his men to the land of the Philistines, whose king gave him a city, Ziklag. From Ziklag, David led nightly raids against the enemies of Israel, convincing the Philistines he was doing it for them. Then one day

If you want to kill giants, follow a giant killer!

the Philistines decided to fight Israel. Many of the men wanted to take David along because of his obvious military strength and prowess. But the princes of the Philistines wouldn't let David go, saying that he would turn on them in the battle and defeat them in order to get back on Saul's good side. After this humiliation, David and his men then returned to Ziklag, only to find it burned and looted by the Amalekites. Every wife, child, and possession was gone.

David's seriously bad day would have been the last straw for most of us. He had been rejected by the king, rejected by the Israelites, and even rejected by their enemies. (You know you've had a bad day when the *devil* rejects you.) But in this moment, David faces the deepest and most betraying rejection of all. At the sight of their burned city and missing families, his mighty men—those he'd turned from disenfranchised to contributing citizens, whom he'd persevered with for years, and whose families he'd protected and provided for—talked about stoning him. Now even the rejected of society had rejected him. David was rejected, and was about to be killed. There really isn't much difference between their attitude and the common prejudice in our society today: If there's a problem, get rid of the guy at the top. But this is a deeper injustice because these men owe their lives to David.

Scripture records what David is feeling in this moment:

> *Now David was greatly distressed, for the people spoke of stoning him, because the soul of all the people was grieved, every man for his sons and his daughters...* (1 Samuel 30:6).

Without question I would feel "greatly distressed" too if my life is threatened by my closest friends. But how does David respond? Does he run for his life? Does he become indignant and start defending his place as their leader by reminding them that they owe him their lives? He easily could have done either, but this is what he did instead:

> *...But David strengthened himself in the Lord his God* (1 Samuel 30:6).

THE BACK DOOR TO THE THRONE ROOM

Facing a volatile group of men ready to stone him caused him not to look to himself for strength but to the Lord his God. His faith gave him the courage to essentially say, "Come on, guys! We've got wives and kids to bring back!" Amazingly, this was all it took to knock the sense back into his men. He simply called them back to the purpose and vision for their lives—demonstrating the true character of a strengthened leader. God gave him the strength to master his own distress, look past the offense of his men's rejection, and rally them together to get their families back. When he turned to the men in strength, they pulled themselves together, went after the Amalekites, and retrieved every person and possession that had been taken. But David's personal breakthrough in this moment, his ability to strengthen himself and be faithful to his purpose instead of collapsing under pressure, not only saved his life, it also enabled him to lead his men to victory. His breakthrough kept him standing in front of an unseen door that was just about to open—the door to the throne room. The very battle the Philistines had just prevented him from fighting was the battle in which Saul and Jonathan died. Only a short time later, Israel crowned David king. His darkest moment led him to the back door of the throne room.

Leaving a Legacy that Lasts

The story, of course, does not end there. The true significance of David's promotion from the field to the throne is seen in his kingly legacy. It would be stunning enough if David had only written the Psalms, established an unprecedented form of worship in Jerusalem, designed the Temple, and brought Israel into its Golden Age; but King David was so important to God that he was named *the* forerunner of the Messiah. Jesus, throughout *eternity*, will be identified as the Son of David and sit on David's throne. David was promoted to a place of such favor and influence with God that he altered the course of history forever.

David's life was not set down in Scripture merely to inspire us. We only need to read the accounts of his sins to know that he was not some kind of superhero. David's life is really a call to every believer. If one man who was a sinner who lived hundreds of years before the blood of Jesus was shed, could come into that place of favor with God, then how much more should those who are covered by that blood be able to come into an even greater destiny—to be like Christ and finish His work on the planet? John describes the destiny we've received in Jesus in Revelation 5:9-10, the destiny all of Heaven is singing about: "*...You were slain, and have redeemed us to God by Your blood out of every tribe and tongue and people and nation, and have made us* ***kings and priests*** *to our God; and we shall reign on the earth.*" As proof that our position as kings and priests is not something less than the position David held, the writer of Ephesians states that we are seated in Christ in heavenly places (see Eph. 2:6). If Jesus is currently seated on the throne of David, then so are we!

We are living in a time when the Lord is restoring this revelation to His people—that the blood of Jesus was not shed merely to save us from our sins, but to restore us to a relationship with God in which we partner with Him as kings and priests to bring the planet under His rule and reign. We have delegated authority to establish His Kingdom wherever the sole of our foot treads. But the fact is, while God calls us "kings," the degree to which we walk in that position is a matter of *potential.* And as Larry Randolph points out, God is not responsible for making us reach our potential. A lot of believers think God is not fulfilling the prophetic words over their lives because they have missed the fact that the word was pointing to their potential, which requires their participation. God won't fulfill your potential because He wants you to become a mature believer who thinks and acts like Him out of your own free will. Mature believers are those He can trust with the secrets of His heart because they will not use the favor He gives for their own purposes, but for His.

Increased Favor Secures our Destiny

Some of us who have been raised in a democratic society may struggle with the idea that God gives more favor to some people than others. God's favor is not the same as His love. You cannot do anything to change the vastness of God's love for you. But even Jesus Himself had to grow "*...in favor with God and man*" (Luke 2:52). This verse amazes me. I can understand the fact that He needed to grow in favor with man, but why did He have to grow in favor with God? He was perfect in every way. The answer lies in the fact that Jesus did everything He did *as a man*, laying His divinity aside, in order to be a model for us. Therefore, He, like David, had to be tested. At His baptism, He received His anointing as the Spirit descended on Him and remained, and He was declared by the Father to be the Son of God. But instead of launching right into His ministry, He was led by the Spirit into the wilderness. There He was tested by the enemy, specifically in the area of the Word that had just been spoken over Him. If you look at the account of Jesus' temptation in Luke, you'll notice that He goes into the wilderness "*filled with the Holy Spirit*" and He returns "*in the power of the Spirit*" (Luke 4:1,14). Because He passed the test, the expression of the word over His life, the favor to walk in His potential, was released in a greater measure.

The "favor" that Jesus grew in is the word *charis*, which refers to the divine grace and ability of God Himself that comes upon and enables a person to accomplish His purposes. As Jesus modeled, each of us must grow in favor if we are going to fulfill our destiny in God. But favor, because it is so glorious and powerful, is a weighty thing. Thus, God, in His mercy, gives you His favor in the measure your character can handle, taking you from glory to glory, faith to faith, and strength to strength.

THE PURPOSE AND PRIORITY OF MINISTERING TO YOURSELF

David's life shows us that the ability to strengthen and minister to ourselves is a vital skill that we must learn if we are going to develop the character to fulfill our potential as kings and priests. It is impossible for anyone to reach his ultimate destiny in life without learning to minister to himself. We can best appreciate the significance of this ability by understanding the nature of the role to which we are called. When Scripture says "*we shall reign on the earth*" (Rev. 5:10), the implication is that every one of us has a destiny to stand in a position where we influence people around us. Each of us will have a different size and kind of sphere of influence, but we are all called as leaders in society. We are not called to "rule over others" in the sense of domination. In God's Kingdom, the power of rule is the divine enablement to serve others more effectively. And just as kings are to provide protection and prosperity for their citizens, so those who serve well in God's Kingdom will offer safety and blessing to all who come under their influence.

Perhaps the first quality that distinguishes a leader is *initiative*. God knew David would succeed as a leader because he took the initiative to seek Him in the secret place. This is the same quality of maturity that He is looking for in us. To experience the positive peer pressure and momentum of a move of God in a corporate group is wonderful. But those who seek God's face and pursue His destiny for their lives when nobody is around, are the people who possess the initiative required to strengthen themselves. If they learn to sustain their initiative to seek God by strengthening themselves in testing, they will be the people who will experience the personal breakthroughs that release a corporate blessing to those around them.

God wants us to learn how to strengthen ourselves through Him because developing our skills will promote spiritual longevity. We need longevity because our destiny and potential cannot be attained in a few years; they extend to the end of our lifetime here on earth. For this reason, I like to tell the students in our School of Supernatural Ministry, "Anyone can burn for God for a year. Come back in twenty years, take me out to coffee, and tell me you're still burning." Then I spend much of the school year teaching them the tools I've learned for strengthening myself. It's obvious that the students possess enough initiative to pay the price to come to school; but without discovering and using tools to minister to themselves, they won't, I'm convinced, be able to sustain the desire that brought them initially. Sadly, I know too many Christian leaders who lack this ability, and as a result are suffering from burnout or moral failure.

Now, let me be clear that learning to strengthen ourselves does not mean that we develop an independent lifestyle. Our lifestyle as believers is always focused on serving, loving, and leaning on the Body of Christ. But for the sake of becoming mature and growing in favor so that we can bless those around us, God brings moments into our lives when we have to stand alone in difficulty and testing. God will even blind the eyes and deafen the ears of our closest friends in those moments so we can learn to minister to ourselves. We must recognize this because I know a lot of believers who fall into bitterness, thinking their friends are failing them in a hard time. Understanding God's priority to teach us this lesson helps us to avoid that trap.

VICTORY AS A LIFESTYLE

This book is written to share the tools that the Lord has taught me to use to strengthen myself. My purpose is not to make an exhaustive list of tools in the Scripture, but to show you the things that have brought me through tough days in the trenches. As you read about the things that God has put in your arsenal, my desire is that the *conviction* of the destiny over your life will be more deeply rooted in your heart. He has equipped you for great victory—not just merely to break through, but to release and establish the dominion of God around you. However, it's your responsibility to use these tools to bring strength to yourself so you can stand in that victory. The invitation of a lifetime is before you—an invitation to walk in a place of favor where you co-labor with God and make history as a king and priest of His choosing. Let's rise to the challenge!

Chapter 2

Staying Connected to Your Destiny

The enemy uses lies to make problems appear bigger than the solutions we carry.

God never sets us up to fail—only to grow.

Keeping tabs on all the different aspects of the Christian life can be overwhelming. There is a seemingly endless list of responsibilities to attend to. There is the issue of relationships inside and outside of our immediate family, our place of employment, ministry, community involvement, and evangelism. And then there's the issue of Christian disciplines like prayer, personal Bible study, witnessing, corporate gatherings, fasting—the list goes on and on. And to make matters worse, most of us are quite capable of making simple things very complex. Yet Jesus illustrated a simple lifestyle: one that is carefree—not irresponsible, but simply without cares. Solomon seemed to recognize a key to this great Kingdom lifestyle when he said, "*Watch over your heart with all diligence, for from it flow the springs of life*" (Prov. 4:23 NASB). All the issues of our lives flow forth like rivers from one central location—the heart—and what we do in stewarding that one place determines the outcome of our lives.

We live in the crossroads daily—that place between mystery and revelation. My job is to trust my heavenly Father with the problems and situations I don't understand, and focus on stewarding my will to what I know to be true. My success in watching over my heart determines the measure of Kingdom breakthrough I will experience in life. In other words, my internal reality often defines the nature of my external reality: if I prosper in my heart, my life will prosper.

Strengthening ourselves in the Lord is an essential part of stewarding our heart. The tools that I have learned to use to strengthen myself in the Lord have become calculated responses to the warning lights of my heart. But the fact is, I can only respond correctly if I already recognize and understand the signals my heart sends. If the oil light comes on in my car, and my response is to take it to the car wash, I clearly do not understand what the light means. Worse yet, the real problem has not been dealt with and will soon manifest in a breakdown. When it comes to my heart, I have found that the only way I can correctly use the tools I've received to strengthen myself is to establish foundational truths in my thinking—truths about the nature of reality, who God is, and who He has made me to be. These truths help me identify my heart signals. I will share some of that thinking in this chapter as context for understanding the tools I use to strengthen myself. I will address those helpful tools in the remainder of the book.

Becoming from Beholding

Did you know that your thinking and your heart are intimately connected? The Western mind-set compartmentalizes human beings when it comes to feelings and thinking—the heart feels and the mind thinks. But Scripture says, "*For as he* ***thinks in his heart,*** *so is he...*" (Prov. 23:7). In fact, the Hebrew definition of the word "heart" encompasses the entirety of your "inner man." Your heart is the seat of your mind, imagination, will, desires, emotions, affections, memory, and conscience. It is also the center of your communion with the Spirit of God and possesses the faculties that perceive spiritual reality. Scripture refers to this spiritual perception as "the eyes of your heart." Thus, your heart is what enables you to have *faith,* which is the "*evidence of things not seen*" (Heb. 11:1). Your faith grows as your heart, led by the Holy Spirit, perceives and understands the invisible realm of spiritual reality. That unseen realm governs the visible realm and brings your mind and will into agreement with the reality of the Kingdom. In essence, what I have just described is the process of renewing the mind.

Our internal *focus* on and agreement with spiritual reality—either the reality of God's Kingdom, established on the truth, or the destructive reality of the enemy's kingdom, established on lies—gives permission for that reality to flow into the "issues of life."

This power of agreement with spiritual reality through our focus adds another dimension to the principle that life flows from the heart: *you become what you behold.* As I said in the previous chapter, God has made clear what we are becoming—the potential we are all called to grow into throughout our lifetime. We are becoming kings and priests of the planet, following the lead of our Elder Brother, Jesus. This is why Hebrews tells us to *fix our eyes on Jesus* (see Heb. 12:2). Our goal is to sustain our focus on Him because we become like the One we behold. The degree to which we understand our identity and purpose—who we are becoming—is always determined by the degree of our revelation of Jesus. He is the exact representation of the Father, in whose image we were created.

Beholding Jesus cannot be reduced to reading about Him in Scripture. He died so that the same Spirit who was in and upon Him, giving Him constant access to what the Father was saying and doing, could be sent to live in us. The truth is that every believer has constant access to the manifest presence of God. We are an open heaven. But we have to take advantage of that access, and we do that by turning our focus on Him. Only in that place of communion with Him do we come to *know* Him, and consequently, gain the revelation of our identity and purpose. And as we agree with the *revelation* of who He is, the *reality* of who He is starts to flow into our lives and transform us into His likeness. All fruitfulness in our lives flows from this place of intimacy with the Lord.

Agreeing with the Unseen

Because our communion with the Lord is the power source of our lives and connects us with our eternal purpose as kings and priests of the planet, the kingdom of darkness is generally aimed at dislodging us from it and getting us to focus on something else. The enemy knows that our job, as we walk in our position of delegated authority, is to destroy his works—to close the distance between the invisible reality of God's Kingdom and the unredeemed reality of our circumstances. The inferior reality of our physical circumstances always yields to the superior reality of the Kingdom—but we can only release that Kingdom to the degree to which our heart and mind are in agreement with it. So the enemy uses lies of accusation and intimidation to make the problems and conflicts in our lives, which result from the incongruence between the heavenly reality and earthly reality, appear bigger than the solutions we carry.

> The enemy uses lies to make problems appear bigger than the solutions we carry.

In the moments when we are confronted by the clash between the seen and the unseen realms, God has an agenda and the enemy has an agenda. We always choose to partner with one or the other. In doing so, we decide whether the situation is a test that proves and strengthens our character and faith to walk in our purpose, showing God that He can entrust us with more of Himself, or whether the situation is a temptation away from God into bitterness, doubt, anxiety, and disappointment. This choice really should be a no-brainer for us. I mean, who cares what the devil's agenda is? God's agenda is so glorious, and His love and purposes for our lives are so great, that everything else pales in comparison. We should all be like Nehemiah, who, when the enemies of Israel tried to get him to come out of the city and talk with them on the Plain of Ono, said, "*...I am doing a great work and I cannot come down. Why should the work cease while I leave it and go down to you?*" (Neh. 6:3).

But the truth is that we can only ignore the enemy when we are firmly convinced that we are doing a great work for God, a work that He has commissioned us to do. Our *co-mission* comes from our *sub-mission* to His primary mission: "*on earth as it is in Heaven.*" Only a passionate devotion to God and an unwavering conviction about the identity and purpose He has given us will be stronger than the enemy's resolve to distract us. If we are not convinced of our purpose, then we will entertain the enemy's lies and invite his destruction into our lives. The key to gaining this conviction and passion is, once again, a sustained focus on the Lord and His Word over us. One of the most poignant explanations in Scripture for why Israel failed to walk in their covenant with God is in Lamentations 1:9: "*...She did not consider her destiny; therefore her collapse was awesome.*" Jerusalem had an awesome destiny. But her failure to consider it led to an awesome collapse. Her destruction was equal in proportion to her potential for greatness. The reason we see human beings capable of great destruction and evil—we are the ones in God's creation who have the greatest potential for greatness. The key to either great purpose or great destruction lies in where we choose to sustain our focus. Knowing this fact should move us to jealously guard our intimacy with the Lord.

PERSONAL VICTORY—CORPORATE BLESSING

You probably noticed this, but the tests that David endured were tests that specifically addressed his ability to keep his focus on his identity and purpose. He was tested by coming into circumstances that directly contradicted God's Word over his life. His job was to ignore the enemy's agenda and develop the strength of character that God was after. It was like God was saying, "OK David, I've called you as a man after my own heart and anointed you to be king of Israel. That is your destiny. Will you be a king with my heart when the man currently in your position is attacking you, chasing you, and doing everything to keep you from your destiny? Will you be that king when the Jews you are supposed to rule intend to turn you over to the enemy? Will you be that king when your army consists of a bunch of losers? Will you be that king when your palace is a cave in the wilderness? And will you be that king when your closest friends disown you and threaten your life? If you can strengthen yourself in

Me, then you can be trusted to be that king when all the circumstances line up."

David's actions prove that He believed God's promises over his life. Likewise, the difficulties in our lives expose the degree to which we really believe that God is for us and that His words about our destiny are true. This is the essence of faith—not intellectual assent to truths; but the practical trust we express in God based on who we know Him to be through our relationship with Him. We express that trust when we choose to listen to Him in the midst of our circumstances more than any other voice and then respond to our circumstances in light of what He has said. The tools that David used to strengthen himself in his tests had to be activities that kept him connected to God and to what God had said, because what he did in these tests was consistent with the word over his life, and released purpose to those around him.

I would venture to say that the things David did to strengthen himself were some of the very same things that he did to connect with the Lord *before* he was brought into the time of testing. He did not go into the wilderness without tools to face the tests he would meet there. God took him there because he was ready—not yet ready for the kingship, but for a series of tests that increased in difficulty as he proved strong enough to handle them. This reveals a truth about the nature of God that should give us good reason to trust Him when we experience challenges in life. That truth—always be prepared for the moment in which you're standing, because God never fails to give you the tools you need beforehand. You can see this aspect of His nature in this episode of the Exodus story:

> *Then it came to pass, when Pharaoh had let the people go, that God did not lead them by way of the land of the Philistines, although that was near; for God said, "Lest perhaps the people change their minds when they see war, and return to Egypt"* (Exodus 13:17).

God kept the Israelites away from a challenge they were not prepared to face. The corollary truth is that the battles and tests He led them into were ones for which He had prepared them. God is a good Father. He never sets us up to fail, but only to grow. Just as I would never send my own children against a challenge they were unprepared to handle, neither does He. God nevers sets us up to fail—only to grow!

God never set us up to fail—only to grow.

The Cornerstone of Revelation—God is Good

I believe that the reason many believers fall into the trap of fear and anxiety in the midst of crisis is because they allow the enemy to successfully distract them from the fact that they are prepared with tools they already have in their arsenal. It's easy for us to feel blindsided by events that we did not expect; but nothing surprises God, which is why He prepares us for what's ahead. Remembering that He has seen ahead and has prepared us is simple, but it makes a huge difference in our response to difficulty. When we have our hearts anchored in this truth about His nature, we will be oriented to take inventory of our tools and start using them when we come up against a challenge. The bedrock of an automatic response from us is the burning conviction that God is good, always good! Doubting His goodness, making up explanations for things we don't understand (the source of a lot of bad theology), or falling into anxiety and disappointment won't be options for us. It's like knowing exactly what to do when the oil light goes on in our car. When the truth of God's goodness is *not* firmly anchored in our hearts, we are not only dislodged from our purpose in conflict, but we don't possess the sensitivity of heart, the faith, to perceive the tools God gives us to prepare us before we encounter a challenge. We learn this lesson from Jesus' disciples. Shortly after they witnessed the miracle of the loaves and fishes, the disciples were in a boat in the middle of a storm on the lake. In the midst of the storm, Jesus walked out on the water to them and stilled the storm. The disciples were overwhelmed by His demonstration of power, their unbelief, and probably their own lack of readiness to face another obstacle with their own authority. Mark gave the following explanation for their reaction: "*For they had not understood about the loaves, because their heart was hardened*" (Mark 6:52). In this season of His ministry, Jesus was training His disciples to do what He did. Every miracle He did in their presence was a lesson about the nature of God and an invitation for them to live from that revelation. In calming the storm He was demonstrating a dimension of God's power and authority that logically connected to the power and authority He had demonstrated earlier in the miracle of the loaves. It's like He had taught them multiplication and was moving on to algebra; but they couldn't move on, because they didn't understand the first lesson.

Why didn't they get the lesson of the loaves? Their hearts were hard. They lacked the basic faith in who God is and they lacked an understanding of the way He works to orient them to learn the lessons He was teaching to prepare them for life and ministry—in this case, facing another storm. What a sobering lesson it is to see that it is possible to be perfectly obedient to the Lord's commands (in obtaining the available food, and in handing it out to the multitudes), be used in bringing forth a miracle, and still not get the tools that God made available because of a hard heart. Jesus' rebuke gave them a chance to repent that they might recover what they had missed in the miracle.

Our ability to connect with what God is doing in the midst of difficult circumstances depends on our ability to remember who He is and what He has done in our lives—our relational history with Him. I guarantee that if you are currently facing a situation that seems beyond your strength or understanding, and you take some time to rehearse your history with the Lord over the last 12 months or so, you will always find a tool—a prophetic word, a Scripture verse that has leapt out at you, a testimony, or a prayer strategy, for example—that God has put in your arsenal, something that provides a key to overcome the present situation. You also might need to repent for any hardness of heart that has kept you from getting what He has made available to you.

As you become more and more convinced that you are a person with a great identity and purpose, that you are prepared for the moment you're standing in, and that all of Heaven is waiting to back you up as you choose to be faithful to your purpose, your perception of which forces are the most operative in your life will shift. That perception will open you up to the lessons about the unseen realities all around you. Such a shift makes learning natural.

Joseph discovered this. As he came into his destiny, he saw that God's plans and purposes had a momentum and power that outweighed the evil plans of his brothers. He said, "*But as for you, you meant evil against me; but God meant it for good, in order to bring it about as it is this day, to save many people alive*" (Gen. 50:20). His statement doesn't deny the reality that his brothers made choices that affected his life, but focuses on the superior reality that their plans couldn't cancel out God's purpose for him. In fact, those evil intentions became the very tools that God used to bring Joseph into his promotion and the ultimate fulfillment of God's promise. While God doesn't create evil, evil does not limit His ability to bring about the fulfillment of all that He has purposed to do in us.

THE BENEFITS OF CONFLICT

This is another reason never to be concerned about what the enemy might be planning. (I'm not denying our need for discernment; but our discernment is never to give undue attention to the devil. It's mainly designed to recognize which channel the enemy's voice is speaking on so we can push the "mute" button.) The devil has never been a threat to God. God could easily wipe out the whole kingdom of darkness in a moment. God decided it would be more beneficial and more glorious to share His victory with sons and daughters made in His image who can put on display what He's like. And He's not above using the devil as a pawn to accomplish His purposes, just as He used Pharaoh as an enemy of Israel. Psalm 105, in recounting the history of Israel's journey to Egypt and their triumphal Exodus, says:

> *He increased His people greatly, and made them stronger than their enemies. He turned their heart to hate His people, to deal craftily with His servants. He sent Moses His servant, and Aaron whom He*

had chosen. They performed His signs among them, and wonders in the land of Ham...He also brought them out with silver and gold, and there was none feeble among His tribes. Egypt was glad when they departed, for the fear of them had fallen upon them (Psalm 105:24-38).

This verse is basically saying that God sent Israel to Egypt so He could pick a fight. He blessed and multiplied His people until they were a threat to the enemy, then went to the enemy, hardened their hearts, and provoked them. This divine setup justified His rising up on behalf of His people, displaying His wonders, pouring out plagues on the Egyptians, and bringing the Israelites out loaded with spoils. What a strategy!

So God not only prepares us for conflict, He leads us right into it. I'm not saying He is the cause of difficulty in our lives. He is not, nor has He ever been, the sort of Father who brings torment, sickness, or persecution into the lives of His children to teach them how to be more Christ-like. The point is that when we are pursuing our God-given purpose, every situation in our lives works together to accomplish it. We never have to live in a moment of conflict without divine purpose because God can win with any hand, even a pair of twos.

In reality, He already *has* won. Our job is to align our hearts with the reality of the victory of the Cross so that we can see His purposes and redemption at work around us. Then we can recognize how to partner with

Heaven in our circumstances. People who have this perspective stand out because they get happy when they encounter a problem. They know it is their assignment, privilege, and joy to see impossibilities and problems bend their knees to the name of Jesus.

THE FRONTLINES OF BATTLE—THE PLACE OF GREATEST SAFETY

While each believer has a different assignment corresponding to his or her unique gifts and talents, these assignments work to accomplish one purpose—the establishment of the Kingdom "*on earth as it is in Heaven.*" This Kingdom, as Scripture says, "*forcefully advances*" (see Matt. 11:12)—first to displace the attitudes of the carnal man in our own lives and then to destroy the works of the devil around us. The violence of this process may seem overwhelming at times, but it is safer to stay in the midst of this conflict than to adopt a defensive, conservative approach to the Christian life. The safest place for us to be at any point in our lives is passionately pursing God and the purposes to which He has called us. Passionate pursuit positions us for advancement. To live in the defensive posture protecting what we have is quite dangerous. Just ask the man who buried his one talent (see Matt. 25:18-28).

Our assignment and destiny is to advance the Kingdom, and comes with an umbrella of grace and favor that works to preserve our lives, no matter what's going on around us. The moment we take a back seat in our pursuit of the Kingdom is the moment we become exposed to fiery darts of deception.

The more we establish these truths about reality in our thinking, the more we will understand the priority of stewarding our hearts. Your destiny begins in your heart. The more you gaze on the face of Jesus with the eyes of your heart, the more you see who you are becoming. The more your energies and thoughts are focused on your destiny, the more your passion and conviction grow: "I am alive to burn for God. I'm alive to make Him known." Your passion and conviction give you a momentum to pursue this one thing, from which all other passions and purposes flow. Your pursuit is the thing that attracts Heaven to bring you into that destiny.

So as I navigate the various challenges and obstacles on the highway to my destiny, I'm watching the warning lights of my heart. I must sustain my connection with the Source of life. Really, there's only one light—the oil light. It's the oil of His presence that gives me everything I need and anoints me to fulfill my purpose. But He only gives me the measure of His presence that I'm willing to jealously guard. So I have to build the strength of will and character to focus all my energies on carrying His presence with excellence. I can't afford to have a moment in my life when the circumstances distract me from tending that fire in my heart—even a situation when I must tend the fire by myself.

Chapter 3

DISARMING HELL THROUGH THANKSGIVING

Thanksgiving keeps us sane and alive.

When you were born again, the desire to please God and do His will became part of your nature. You don't have to work it up; it comes naturally. What many believers don't know is that God did not put that desire in us and then make His will something so obscure that we couldn't discover and accomplish it. The will of God instinctively becomes the will of believers through intimate relationship with Jesus Christ.

The will of God is not complicated. Many young people ask me to pray for them saying, "I just want to know what God's will is for my life." I often tell them that I already know what God's will is. It is found in the Lord's Prayer: "*Your will be done on earth as it is in heaven*" (Matt. 6:10). God's will is simply for Heaven's reality to become earth's reality.

Our Role in Fulfilling "*As It Is in Heaven*"

We are God's delegated authority. As such, our obedience plays an important role in seeing the will of

God accomplished on the earth. In First Thessalonians 5:16-18, Paul instructs us to: "*Rejoice always, pray without ceasing, in everything give thanks;* ***for this is the will of God*** *in Christ Jesus for you.*" Two things in this statement stand out. First of all, the will of God is not merely focused on whether we become a doctor or a teacher or whether we're supposed to have tuna or peanut butter for lunch. It is focused on what we do to position our heart in relationship to God at all times, in all circumstances. Secondly, rejoicing, praying and thanksgiving are all acts of *our* will that, particularly in times of difficulty, weakness and uncertainty, require faith. They are activities that draw our focus to Heaven so we can agree with what is true, no matter what we feel or perceive with our physical senses and emotions. And since our agreement is what attracts the strength and reality of Heaven into our lives and circumstances, it makes sense that these activities fulfill the will of God expressed in the Lord's Prayer—*on earth as it is in Heaven.* The transformation of the heart is the first step in bringing heaven to earth.

Because rejoicing, prayer, and thanksgiving attract heaven; they are vital tools for strengthening ourselves in the Lord. You'll notice that all of them are meant to be continuously ongoing in our lives. They're not reserved for crises or holidays. They're a lifestyle—as are all the tools that we use to minister to ourselves. A big reason for this is that in the midst of crisis and difficulty, it is usually hard if not impossible to sit down and reason out how we should respond. Difficulty has a way of exposing the degree to which our lives and minds have been truly transformed by a heavenly perspective for certain responses to be habitual. The things we practice as a lifestyle equip us for difficulties.

In the next two chapters I share some of the ways that the Lord has taught me to *rejoice* and *pray*, as well as the insights I've gained about how and why these things bring strength. But here I'm going to talk about *thanksgiving.*

Thanksgiving agrees with Heaven by acknowledging the truth that our lives are a gift from God, and that He is sovereign over all. God is extravagantly generous, and the life He has given us to experience on this planet is not a life of survival, but of abundance and blessing. But unless we properly recognize what we've been given, we won't be able to experience that life. That's the reality of receiving a gift. If we don't understand what we've been given, we won't understand its purpose and be able to experience its benefit.

Imagine Christmas morning. You've spent the last few months shopping and picking out unique gifts for each of your family members that show your intimate knowledge of their interests and desires. You have spared no expense to get gifts of the highest quality that will be both enjoyable and beneficial to each person. But when your family comes to the Christmas tree, one person completely ignores the presents. Another person opens your gift, but starts using it for something other than what it was made for. Still another just holds the gift, and refuses to unwrap it.

And to make matters worse, none of them even acknowledge that their gifts are from you. Can you see how these responses are not only foolish, but are deeply harmful to the relationship?

Sadly, this is how many Christians respond to God's gifts, particularly the gifts of the Spirit. So many people fail to receive what the Lord has offered them because they don't understand what the gifts are or how to use them. They say ridiculous things like, "Well, tongues is the least of the gifts, so I don't need to pursue it." If my children said this about one of the presents I had put under the tree for them, I'd be very upset. I'd say, "This is yours! I don't care how small you think it is. I bought it with you in mind, and I don't give cheap gifts. If you'll just open it, I'll show you what it is and how to use it." Such a rejection of gifts is absolute arrogance.

Thankfulness carries an attitude of humility. Thanksgiving is the only proper way to receive what God has given us because it honors our relationship with Him by expressing trust in His goodness, even if we don't yet understand what we've received. God gives us "every good and perfect gift" for two primary reasons. He gives to make us prosper so we can succeed in life, and He gives to demonstrate His love as an invitation to relationship. When we practice thanksgiving as a lifestyle, we recognize that the gifts we have received from the Lord came with these purposes. Thanksgiving sets us on a course to know God in relationship and discover the reasons for which He made us.

THE GREAT PRICE OF LITTLE THANKS

When God tells us to give Him thanks, He's not insinuating that He gives in order to get something from us. He doesn't manipulate us with His gifts. He wants us to thank Him because thankfulness acknowledges the truth about our lives. And when we agree with the truth, then the truth sets us free to see and manifest the greatness that He has put in us as the ones He has made in His image. When we withhold thanks from God, we actually cut ourselves off from who we are. This is what Paul explains in Romans 1:18-21.

> *For the wrath of God is revealed from heaven against all ungodliness and unrighteousness of men, who suppress the truth in unrighteousness...so that they are without excuse, because, although they knew God, they did not glorify Him as God,* ***nor were thankful****, but became futile in their thoughts, and their foolish hearts were darkened.*

Paul is basically saying that God has not kept who He is a secret. Knowing God is not hard. It's actually the most obvious thing in the world. All you have to do is glorify Him as God and be thankful. This response, because it agrees with the truth, gives you open access to the vast treasures of the knowledge of God. But without that response, your thoughts become *futile* and your heart is *darkened.* Futile means "purposeless." When we fail to sustain the response of thanksgiving for everything in our lives, our thinking is cut off from our purpose in God. When we lose sight of our purpose, we will inevitably make choices that are outside of God's intentions for our lives, and this can only be destructive because it works against His design for us. A dark heart is a heart that is unable to perceive spiritual reality. It is unmoved by the desires and affections of the Lord, and therefore cannot respond to His invitation to relationship, which is the source of life. As Paul goes on to explain in Romans chapter 1, a dark heart perverts our desires and leads us into all kinds of sin that degrades our identity and relationships. The most perverted sins known to mankind came about through a door left open because of the absence of thankfulness.

The Purifying Nature of Thankfulness

Since thanksgiving keeps us sane and alive by connecting us to the source of our life and purpose, it makes sense that Paul instructs us to give thanks "*in everything*." Thanksgiving keeps us sane and alive. But there is a specific dimension of thanksgiving that is particularly powerful in times of difficulty and adversity. We find this principle in Paul's first letter to Timothy.

> Thanksgiving keeps us sane and alive.

Now the Spirit expressly says that in latter times some will depart from the faith, giving heed to

> *deceiving spirits and doctrines of demons...commanding to abstain from foods which God created to be received with thanksgiving by those who believe and know the truth. For every creature of God is good, and nothing is to be refused if it is received with thanksgiving; for it is sanctified by the word of God and prayer* (1 Timothy 4:1-5).

Food was one of the biggest "disputable matters" that the early Church struggled with, particularly regarding the issue of eating food offered to idols. Jewish and Gentile believers alike feared that this food was defiled by having been dedicated to demonic spirits. False teachers of the time preyed upon this superstition and caused all kinds of bondage and division. Interestingly, in this passage Paul doesn't debunk the superstition and say that dedicating food to idols is powerless. He simply says that combining thanksgiving with the Word and prayer is powerful enough to deauthorize that dedication and create a stronger one—a dedication to the Lord. He is saying thanksgiving *sanctifies* whatever it touches.

Sanctification is a significant subject throughout Scripture. In the Old Testament it was primarily associated with the specific rituals God prescribed for setting aside various instruments, vessels, and pieces of furniture for priestly use in the Tabernacle of Moses, and later the Temple of Solomon. After a goldsmith had finished fashioning a bowl for use in the sacrifices, for example, it would be sprinkled with blood from the altar. From that point on, it would never be used for anything but priestly service in the Temple. It was completely set apart for God—sanctified. In the New Testament, believers are sanctified by the Blood of Jesus and set apart for God. This sanctification is even more powerful, because we do not merely become vessels that He can use to accomplish His purposes. The very process by which His life, power and love flow through us is the process that transforms us into His likeness. We become *like* the One with whom we are set apart.

When Paul says that thanksgiving sanctifies unclean food, he is saying that it sets it apart for God and His purposes. Thanksgiving actually changes the very nature of the food into something holy. This truth extends beyond unclean food. It extends to every situation in your life in which you find other powers at work besides the power of God. It's vital to remember that not everything that happens in life is His will. He didn't cause the crisis a nation or individual may be facing. He actually *can't* give things that are not good because He doesn't have them. Someone can only give what he has. God only gives good gifts, because He is good, and has only good gifts to give. So giving thanks in everything does not mean saying that the adversity came from God. But giving thanks in the midst of an adverse situation, a difficulty intended to undermine your faith and destroy you, enables you to take hold of that situation and set it apart to God and His purposes. When you give thanks, the weapon the enemy meant to use to dislodge you from your divine purpose is put into your hands and becomes the very thing that brings you more fully into that purpose. Jesus declared that He sends us out with the same assignment the Father gave to Him—to destroy the works of the devil (see 1 John 3:8). Thanksgiving accomplishes the divine justice of the Kingdom, where the enemy is destroyed by the very thing he intended to use for our destruction. Just knowing that we can participate in destroying the enemy's purposes should alone move us to give thanks!

Releasing Justice

One of the clearest examples of divine justice in Scripture is found in the Book of Esther: the story of Haman, who was hung on the very gallows he built to destroy Mordecai. Later, this justice was made even more complete when Mordecai assumed Haman's position in the king's court. The wonderful thing about this story is that Mordecai didn't have to bring justice himself. He simply kept his focus on his duty to the heathen king and to his people. This is the nature of warfare in the Kingdom. We don't battle by focusing on the devil. We keep our focus on the King and His Kingdom, and the devil cannot help but be unseated by God's ever-increasing government released through our lives, which illustrates another reason why thanksgiving is powerful in times of adversity. Psalm 100:4 says that we "*enter into His gates with thanksgiving.*" Thanksgiving brings us into the manifest presence of

God and connects us with what He is doing and saying in the midst of our circumstances. Thanksgiving helps to establish our focus on Him so that our awareness shifts from earthly reality to heavenly reality—which we must do in order to release the strength of Heaven into our circumstances.

Keeping My Awareness of God

I have purposed to try to live in such a way that nothing ever gets bigger than my consciousness of God's presence. Sometimes conflict can be as simple as bad news on TV. If it starts to weigh on my heart and grow bigger than my awareness of God, I consciously turn my affection toward Him to become more aware of His presence. If that doesn't work, I turn off the TV or leave the room to redirect my focus until my awareness of Him is bigger than that which weighs heavily on my heart. I can't just know in my head that He's bigger; I have to have my entire being in a position where I am aware of His presence and expect His world to invade my life and circumstances. If I don't sustain this expectation, I will expect other forces to be the prime movers in my life and will begin to live defensively instead of offensively.

When I stay close to the presence of God through thanksgiving, I not only become aware of His absolute ability to invade the impossible, I sense His radical love and delight in me! As I give thanks for the good gifts He's put in my life, I present convincing evidence that He is my Father, He is for me, and His opinion pretty much cancels out all the others. The wonderful thing is that when we simply begin to give thanks, even when it seems difficult to remember one answered prayer, it isn't too long before our *focus* on the good in our lives creates an opening for the Lord's joy. And it's the joy of the Lord that is our strength. I believe that James was talking about giving thanks when he said to *count* it all joy in trial, because giving thanks usually includes taking an inventory of God's gifts in your life. Do the math! If you want to discover the ability of thankfulness to bring you strength in difficulty, you need to keep *counting* these things *until* you come to the conclusion—it's time to rejoice! It becomes really hard to stay depressed about your circumstances when you're filled with the awareness of the love and goodness of God that surrounds and infuses your life.

There is a level of life we can reach where we practice thanksgiving as a lifestyle—a place where we remember our answered prayers. When difficulty comes along, we have a huge inventory of blessings instantly accessible to bring us into His presence as well as the joy and delight He has over us. That is a reality far greater than any accusation, crisis, or conflict that could come our way. When we learn to live in this realm, nothing can deflect us from our purpose. We even make the enemy help us get it done. From Heaven's perspective, it is reasonable to give thanks "in everything"!

Chapter 4

The Personal Breakthrough Moment

Physical obedience brings spiritual breakthrough.

As a young pastor in Weaverville I had more than my share of "Blue Mondays." No matter what wonderful things had happened on Sunday, sometimes all I could remember was what had been lacking in the services. My slides into discouragement were fueled by the comparisons I made between my spiritual heroes and myself. I've always loved reading about revivalists and great men and women of faith—people like John G. Lake, Charles Finney, or Rees Howells. But when I started comparing myself to them, I found that my faith always came up short, and it wouldn't be long before I went into an emotional tailspin over the obvious differences between me and them. Reading the amazing book by Rees Howells, *Intercessor,* made me wonder if I was even breathing, let alone saved. The focus on my limitations didn't help me feel better especially when there were real problems to deal with as a pastor.

Betrayal, abandonment, rejection, and accusation all seemed to come with the position. I often felt like there was a huge black cloud over me. I had enough sense to know that discouragement and depression were not good things. Although I managed to get victory before the next Sunday, because I did carry the conviction that our time together in the house of the Lord was to be a day of celebration, I didn't know how to live that way. Yet.

The Ultimate Priority

One of the priorities that had already been established in my heart as a young man was the priority of worship. My father trained our family and his congregation that our identity as believers is first as worshipers. This meant that our main job was ministering to the Lord, and that everything we did in ministry to people should be an overflow and outgrowth of that primary ministry. Not only that, but he taught and demonstrated that we are to model our praise and worship according to the definition and description in the Psalms, which includes physical expression, like dancing, shouting, clapping, leaping, and making a joyful noise. Emphasizing biblical patterns of worship constituted a big paradigm shift in normal church at the time. At the beginning of this shift many people were resistant to such displays. They were entrenched in the idea that weeping and looking serious were the only genuine manifestations of true spirituality. I agreed with my dad that we should do the stuff in the

Book, but my problem was stepping out of my "reserved personality" box—that is until I realized that God commands us to do it, and that He wouldn't command us to do something that He didn't put in our new nature. That means my real personality in Christ includes the capacity to demonstrate my love for God through biblically mandated expressions. It's who I am. To allow my self-image of being reserved and quiet to rob me of experiencing my new nature that is free to outwardly express my joy in God is a spiritual injustice. I am not willing to come into an agreement with that lie. As a result, I began to dance before the Lord with joy in private long before I had seen anyone do it in a service.

As I discovered, praise isn't pleasing to the flesh, which may be one reason why it's so powerful in removing that cloud of oppression. The enemy is empowered by human agreement. To agree with anything he says gives him a place to kill, steal, and destroy. We fuel the cloud of oppression by agreeing with our enemy. Praise, with rejoicing, cancels that agreement.

INTROSPECTION KILLS THE LIFE OF PRAISE

Praise was one of the primary tools that God had equipped me with as a young man to strengthen myself in the discouragement of my early years as a pastor. I could be questioning a million things about my life, but I never had to question whether I was in the right place when I was giving God praise. It became my default when I slid into the fog of confusion and depression. In Weaverville, our home was behind the church so I often went to the sanctuary late at night, put worship music on the sound system, and spent time praising and worshiping God. Sometimes I remained until early in the morning. I danced, shouted, and basically required myself to do whatever I didn't *feel* like doing. The Psalmist David wrote, "*Bless the Lord, O my soul.*" He commands his own soul to come into order and give God glory. It's important that we learn how to bring our soul, and even our bodies into submission to the purposes of God. Back then I would make sure that the intensity of my praise was in equal proportion to the size of the cloud over my head. Every time, there would come a point when something inside of me would shift, and I was no longer making an effort. My mind, will, emotions, and body were completely filled with conviction of what I was declaring to the Lord. I also noticed that the cloud over my head had disappeared and I was alive in God!

I came to understand that the cloud wasn't just *over* my head; it was *inside* it. I mistakenly thought that focusing on my lack and comparing myself to others was a posture of humility. In fact, it was the opposite. Instead of focusing on God's greatness in my life, I was focusing on myself. I was actually agreeing with the enemy by making my own problems bigger than God's promises. And my agreement invited that cloud of oppression to hover over me.

The only way to break an agreement with a lie is *repentance*, which means to change the way you think. In that place of praise, I fed my mind on the truth of God's nature *until* it created a new agreement with heavenly reality. When that agreement was established, the reality started to manifest in my emotions, mind, and body. But I also came to understand more deeply why my dad taught us to *do* what the Scripture said regarding praise. Making an agreement with Heaven actually requires more than repentance of the mind. You need physical proof to make repentance a legally binding reality. By lining my physical body up with what the Word said, I brought my whole being into agreement with the truth. In doing so, I experienced the principle that physical obedience brings spiritual breakthrough. This may seem a little backward to those of us who hate the idea of going through religious motions and desire to be "authentic" in our worship. Physical obedience bring spiritual breakthrough. But the measure of authenticity is not what you're feeling or thinking. Those things either line up with authentic reality or they don't. And if they don't, Scripture tells us that we get there by *moving*. Some say it's hypocritical to do something you don't feel like doing. I think it's hypocritical

Physical obedience brings spiritual breakgthrough.

to do only what I feel like doing and call myself a believing believer. Right actions release right emotions and right thinking.

But why is it right to sing, shout, dance and leap? Why does God seem to want these radical expressions more than silent, awed reverence? While there is certainly a time for the latter, acts of *celebration* get way more press in the psalmist's descriptions of how we approach God. The reason—God is a God to celebrate. His every action and thought toward us are extravagant expressions of His love, kindness, goodness, and delight in us; and He gives it all not only to bless us for a moment, but to invite us into the deeper blessing of knowing Him. He delights in us, so He wants us to delight in Him. He rejoices over us with singing (see Zeph. 3:17), so He wants us to rejoice in Him with singing. When we give to Him what He gives to us, we step further into relationship with Him, deepening our heart-connection with the source of life.

Not only that, but when we do what He is doing, aligning our bodies as well as our spirits and souls with what He has said, there is a release of His nature that flows to us in that place of intimacy. The Holy Spirit is the most joyful person in existence, and joy is one of the primary expressions of His Kingdom in our lives (see Rom. 14:17). His command to "rejoice always" is really an expression of His desire for us to have joy! He is simply telling us how to receive it. We not only rejoice *because* we have joy—we rejoice in our *pursuit* of joy.

THE IMPORTANCE OF MINISTERING TO GOD

In the previous chapter, I explained that thanksgiving should naturally lead to rejoicing when we follow James' instruction to "*count it all joy.*" As we count up all that God has done, we shouldn't stop at merely thanking God. In every one of the acts of God is a revelation of His nature. And as we see God's nature—His extravagance, joy, love, faithfulness, goodness, and power—the only sensible response is to praise Him. Praise and rejoicing are two sides of the same coin, as we see in Psalm 9:2: "*I will be glad and rejoice in You; I will sing praise to Your name, O Most High.*" It's hard to praise effectively without rejoicing, without bringing our body, soul, and spirit into an expression of celebration. We can't rejoice without having a reason, and that reason is God's nature, revealed in His relationship with us, that we declare in our praises. When God says to "rejoice always," the implication is that we are to establish praise as a lifestyle.

The praise that flows from thanksgiving is described in Hebrews 13:15 as a "sacrifice." This verse gives us a guideline for what kind of activities genuinely qualify as praise. First of all, praise should cost us something. Only then is it a proper response to the God who has given us the costly gift of His own Son. When I forced myself to rejoice in those nights alone in the sanctuary, I was offering God my time, my focus, and my comfort. I was stepping beyond what was convenient and beyond all the pressures of my circumstances. That is what made the act of praise a costly expression. Secondly, a sacrifice of praise should always require faith because it's impossible to please Him apart from faith. Hebrews 11:4 explains that it was "***By faith*** *Abel offered to God a more excellent sacrifice than Cain....*"

It certainly requires faith to rejoice when that's the last thing you feel like doing or seems to make sense in the face of your present circumstances. It doesn't take much faith to hang your head and sing "Thou Art Worthy" when you're really just thinking, "I am worthless!" Truly rejoicing in Him requires that you stand on the truth that you are already accepted by Him where you are. Rejoicing requires you to acknowledge that His goodness and faithfulness are more real than your present difficulty. It especially requires you to agree that your life is not really about you!

Only the rejoicing that requires you to agree with God's perspective on your situation is the sacrifice of praise that pleases Him and has the power to transform you. It is the expression of faith. Sometimes that rejoicing is what David describes in Psalm 2:11: "*rejoice with trembling.*" In other words, you don't have to feel full of faith to rejoice—you just have to do it.

While the nature of praise and thanksgiving is different, they should always go together, because they are sequential steps toward strengthening ourselves in His manifest presence. Psalm 100:4 says we "*enter into His gates with thanksgiving, and into His courts with praise.*" This verse is a road map into the presence of God. Thus, our goal should be to sustain thanks and praise until our whole being is alive to His presence. But we also have to remember in that moment that the focus doesn't change from ministering to God to our getting what we need.

Thanksgiving and praise are tools to strengthen ourselves not because they help us get something from the Lord, but because they reconnect us to our primary purpose—to minister to Him in worship. They bring us into His presence; and true worship is something that only happens in that place of communion with His presence. In worship, the sacrifice is no longer physical expression or verbal declarations. We *are* the sacrifice. Fire always falls on sacrifice. And when we are the sacrifice, we cannot help but be changed.

The Sacrifice that Makes You Rich

Remember the woman with the alabaster vial of perfume who ministered to Jesus? Scripture tells us two things about this vial: it was worth a year's wages (probably this woman's only financial security), and it could only be used on one occasion—because it was in a container that had to be broken to be opened. Not only did she pour the entire contents on Jesus, she did it in a very public display of affection, weeping over His feet and wiping them with her hair. This extreme act provoked extreme offense in all who were present, including His disciples. They were embarrassed by her emotion and disgusted by the waste of money. But Jesus had a different perspective and response. He explained that she had anointed Him for His burial, crediting her with more insight into His true identity than anyone else. She had given Him exactly the kind of worship He deserved, thereby demonstrating faith. And not only that, when everyone left the house, Jesus wasn't the only one drenched in the beautiful fragrance—the aroma encircled the woman as well.

This is what happens when we worship. We don't come to worship saying, "I'm giving this to you so we can share it." Like the woman, we worship to say, "Everything is yours, God." But we can't come from that place of communion with Him without having who He is rub off on us. David said that He is our glory and the lifter of our heads (see Ps. 3:3). We can't be with Him without having our heads lifted to see Him. And you can't look at Him and then look back at your circumstances with the same perspective. Also, you can't experience the realm of His glory, which is His realm of supernatural provision, without receiving a measure of His grace and strength.

One of the primary ways that many believers need to be renewed in their perspective is by getting rid of the idea that intentionally ignoring the problems around them, and even within them, in order to give God praise and thanks, is irresponsible. Believers often fall into the trap of thinking they can find a solution by looking at a problem from every angle and letting it consume their world. But what happens is that the affections of their hearts get drawn away from the Lord, to the point that they care more about the problem than about giving Him what He deserves. They are letting other voices speak louder than His, and that is always irresponsible!

I am responsible to Him first, and for this reason, I have decided to live in a healthy state of denial. When the devil puts a request for attention across my desk, I say, "REQUEST DENIED!" I am aware that there are situations constantly around me that, if I'm not careful, can bring me into discouragement. Most of the time I'm living about 15 minutes away from discouragement if I make a series of wrong choices. But I also know that I never again have to live with discouragement like I used to. I have learned to ignore problems just enough so they don't become a threat to the affections of my heart. I know I'm not being irresponsible because God has promised me over and over that if I'm faithful to be who He has called me to be, especially as a worshiper, He is more than happy to bring the solutions. This does not mean we are not to give attention to problems—but we need to address them from God's perspective.

PRAISE BRINGS A DIVINE ENCOUNTER

Here are a just a couple of the promises in Scriptures regarding the benefits we receive when we're faithful to give Him praise and worship. Psalm 22:3 declares, "*You are holy, enthroned in the praises of Israel.*" Our praises actually create a platform in our circumstances for the King to sit on His throne and release the reality of His Kingdom. And when the Kingdom comes, it always destroys the kingdom of darkness. This is how Isaiah describes it:

> *Sing to the Lord a new song, and His praise from the ends of the earth, you who go down to the sea, and all that is in it, you coastlands and you inhabitants of them! Let the wilderness and its cities lift up their voice, the villages that Kedar inhabits. Let the inhabitants of Sela sing, let them shout from the top of the mountains. Let them give glory to the Lord, and declare His praise in the coastlands. The Lord shall go forth like a mighty man; He shall stir up His zeal like a man of war. He shall cry out, yes, shout aloud; He shall prevail against His enemies* (Isaiah 42:10-13).

He's basically saying that while Israel is celebrating and praising God, God is taking it upon Himself to go out and destroy their enemies. What a deal! This is what happens when God is enthroned in our praises. For example, I can't keep count of all the testimonies I've heard of people who were lost in the presence of God in worship, and only afterward realized that they had been healed. After one service, two individuals, unrelated to each other, came and told me that they had been healed of the lingering effects of a broken neck they had suffered many years earlier. They were both sitting in the same section of the sanctuary, and both were healed during worship!

If those people happened to be rejoicing "with trembling," God certainly gave them yet another good reason to rejoice in Him with real joy. He is more than ready to convince us that He is worthy of our praise. But more than that, He is hoping we'll respond to His invitation to walk in a mature relationship with Him, one in which our primary focus, like His, is not on *getting* but *giving*. Times of difficulty give us an opportunity we don't have otherwise, and that is the opportunity to demonstrate sacrificial love to Him by ministering to Him instead of attending to our pressing needs. In those times we give Him praise solely because we are convinced that knowing Him is the reason to rejoice. When He sees that singleness of heart for Him, that total abandonment, He can't stay away. This kind of relationship is what makes strengthening yourself in the Lord completely opposed to self-sufficiency. It works according to the logic of the Kingdom, which says that you must lose your life to save it. You must give in order to receive. If you need strength, you give yourself so totally to the Lord and His purposes that the Lord becomes the only One who can give you the supernatural strength you need.

So I challenge you to take the time each day to look past the problems and needs around you long enough to give God an extravagant expression of praise and rejoicing. I promise you'll discover that while His blessings are awesome, *He* is the greatest blessing of all. You might also happen to realize that you're becoming a joyful person. After all, God is in a good mood. If you hang around Him, His joy is bound to rub off!

Chapter 5

Releasing the Hidden Things

He is transforming a decent little cottage into a palace He can live in!

One of the most powerful metaphors for the people of God throughout the Scriptures is that we are the *house of God.* The reality that the blood of Jesus made a way for the Spirit of God Himself to dwell inside us is absolutely mind-boggling. But, God moved into a house that needs to be gutted and remodeled, so to speak. Thus, the moment we choose to follow Christ, we sign up for an ongoing process of transformation in our lives that works to change us into a house that can truly express the glory and nature of God in the world. Peter puts it like this: "*You also, as living stones, are being built up a spiritual house, a holy priesthood, to offer up spiritual sacrifices acceptable to God through Jesus Christ*" (1 Peter 2:5). Paul explains in Romans 12:1-2 that this ongoing transformation is taking place primarily in the dimensions of our mind, which must be renewed, and our body, which must be given as a "living sacrifice." The reason—without a yielded heart, a renewed mind, and surrendered body, we can't fully cooperate with the Holy Spirit, who is the Architect and Builder at work in our lives. C.S. Lewis describes this building process in *Mere Christianity*:

> Imagine yourself as a living house. God comes in to rebuild that house. At first, perhaps, you can understand what He is doing. He is getting the drains right and stopping the leaks in the roof and so on: you knew that those jobs needed doing and so you are not surprised. But presently He starts knocking the house about in a way that hurts abominably and does not seem to make sense. What on earth is He up to? The explanation is that He is building quite a different house from the one you thought of—throwing out a new wing here, putting on an extra floor here, running up towers, making courtyards. You thought you were going to be made into a decent little cottage: but He is building a palace. He intends to come and live in it himself.[1]

He is transforming a decent little cottage into a palace.

The key in this illustration is that we must come to understand the "explanation" of what God is doing—His purposes in transforming us. If our minds are not renewed to cooperate with His purposes, we will still be using the "stinking thinking" of our carnal man, which, as Paul tells us, is "*enmity against God*" (Rom. 8:7). It is a sobering thing, but we either have our minds renewed, and become co-laborers with the Lord, or our minds are set against Him! There is no neutral ground. Rejecting the mind of Christ quenches the Holy Spirit and sabotages the building He is doing in our lives. He is transforming a decent little cottage into a palace He can live in!

BUILDING THE BUILDING OF DIVINE PURPOSE

As we've already seen, strengthening ourselves in the Lord is focused on bringing our hearts, minds, and bodies in line with the purposes of God, which results in our having the strength to be true to that purpose in the face of difficulty and opposition. The very word "strengthening" is part of the language of building that is going on our lives. Interestingly, for the most part in the New Testament, we are not doing the building. God is doing the building, as are the men and women He has commissioned to disciple His body. For example, Paul describes himself as a "masterbuilder" who laid the spiritual foundations of the house of God, the community of the redeemed, in Corinth (see 1 Cor. 3:10). However, there are two specific verses that describe something that we do to build ourselves. Jude writes, "*But you, beloved, building yourselves up on your most holy faith, praying in the Holy Spirit*" (Jude 1:20). I believe that "praying in the Holy

Spirit" here specifically refers to praying in tongues, and that Jude is associating this particular activity with building ourselves up in our faith. The reason I believe this is because the same idea is expressed in First Corinthians 14:4: "*He who speaks in a tongue edifies himself....*" The word "edify" means to *build up*. We get the word "edifice" from the same root. As Lance Wallnau teaches, when we pray in tongues, we are constructing an internal edifice of faith from which the purposes of God become manifest.

How does praying in tongues build us up in our faith? To answer this we must first understand what we are doing when we pray in tongues. Paul explains, "*For he who speaks in a tongue does not speak to men but to God, for no one understands him; however, in the spirit he speaks mysteries*" (1 Cor. 14:2). When we speak in tongues, we are using our voices to give utterance to the expressions of our spirits as they commune with the Holy Spirit. This is powerful because our spirits pray in perfect agreement with God because they speak from the new nature we received when we were born again. By engaging our soul, along with our physical body in what our spirits are saying, we come more completely into agreement with the Holy Spirit. As we sustain this prayer, it leads to the same breakthrough we experience when we physically express praise—we become aware of the manifest presence of God. Or, you could say that our bodies and minds begin to experience an increased measure of the reality that our spirits already experience in the Lord's presence.

Unveiling Secrets Through Prayer

In particular, praying in the Spirit gives us access to the reality that the Holy Spirit is teaching us how to think and pray. Jesus explained to His disciples that after He ascended, the Father would send the Spirit for this specific purpose:

> *However, when He, the Spirit of truth, has come, He will guide you into all truth; for He will not speak on His own authority, but whatever He hears He will speak; and He will tell you things to come. He will glorify Me, for He will take of what is Mine and declare it to you* (John 16:13-14).

This is a glorious promise, but we have to understand that the Holy Spirit is not speaking on a megaphone, nor is His the only voice vying for our attention. In order to connect our minds to the frequency on which He is speaking, we have to take a posture of listening by dialing down the voice of our own thoughts and waiting to hear Him. I call it *leaning into His voice.* Praying in tongues is a powerful tool that can turn our focus from the things that distract us, while at the same time help us to become aware of His presence and lean into His voice.

This posture invites the Spirit of revelation to enlighten the "*eyes of our understanding*" (see Eph. 1:18). Understanding is something every person naturally desires to have. We especially want to understand the reasons for things that happen in life, particularly in times of tragedy and crisis. It is never legal to make up our own reasons when we can't seem to reconcile our understanding of Scripture with what we see around us. Sometimes pastors and others in ministry fall to this pressure by trying to give an explanation to something that God is not explaining. Much bad theology is created in such times of pressure—it pleases man by bringing an artificial peace, but is not found in the nature of God.

Scripture first gives us the comfort that when we don't know how to pray, the Holy Spirit Himself prays for us (Rom. 8:26). But then He also gives us the wonderful gift of tongues, which allows us to pray in agreement with the Lord when we lack understanding. Moreover, by drawing us into an awareness of the Lord's presence where our minds perceive what the Spirit is saying, praying in the Spirit actually gives us access to the understanding we need.

When we move into praying with understanding as well as praying with the Spirit, as Paul instructed (1 Cor. 14:14), we further increase the level of our agreement with God in prayer. The fact that praying in the Spirit increases our ability to agree with God in prayer is the key to understanding how praying in the Spirit builds our faith. Praying in tongues bypasses the human intellect and immediately activates our Spirit born faith: for faith does not come from the mind. The link between our level of agreement with Heaven and the level of faith we demonstrate is seen most clearly in Jesus' ministry and in His explanation for how He did what He did. He simply said that He only did what He saw His Father do and said what He heard His Father say (see John 5:19; 12:49). Because everything He did and said was in complete agreement with His Father, everything He did and said was done with faith that released the reality of His Father's Kingdom into the circumstances around Him. That kind of constant connection to the presence of God, which sustains an increasing understanding of who God is and the way He moves, is the heart of faith for the believer. The end result is that we can actually start to think and act like Him.

PRAYING WITH GOD

For this reason, the most effective life of prayer to which God has called us is not a life of throwing up prayer requests and hoping that one will bring an answer. The prayer of faith that always gets results is the kind we can pray because we have drawn close to His heart and heard Him talk about what He wants to do. Then we can stand in the place of delegated authority as a co-laborer and declare what He had said over our circumstances. Asking God to swoop down and fix the problems in our lives does not take the kind of faith God is looking for. The disciples discovered this when they woke up Jesus to do something about a life-threatening storm they were in. First, they asked the Savior of the world a pretty dumb question: "*...Do you not care that we are perishing?*" (Mark 4:38). Then they watched in awe as He fixed their problem.

What caught them even more off guard was that, after answering their prayer, He turned and rebuked them for their lack of faith. The reality is that most anyone cries out to God for help when he's desperate. But desperation is not always an expression of faith. What God was looking for was the kind of faith that would enable them to enforce the will of God through declaration. It is mountain-moving faith, or in this case, storm-canceling faith.

Remember that Scripture is very clear about the plan the Holy Spirit is following as He builds us into His house. If we'll cooperate with Him, we'll start to look just like Jesus. For this reason, I believe God desires every believer to mature to the place where we increasingly see what the Father is doing, hear what He's saying, and step out in faith to agree with Him, just as Christ did. And one of the first gifts the Spirit gives to believers to release the hidden things is the ability to pray in tongues because He knows we need this tool to train our hearts, minds, and bodies to perceive and agree with what He's doing. As you learn how to "build yourself up on your most holy faith" using this tool, a sign of growth will be that God will gradually wean you away from expecting Him to bring quick fixes. Instead, you'll find yourself in situations that simply *will not* shift until you lean into His voice, hear what He's saying, and stand in faith to make that declaration over your life. And as we learn to do this, we find that while getting answers to prayer is wonderful and important, hearing His voice in the intimacy of prayer is the true source of our strength and life.

ENDNOTE

1. C.S. Lewis, *Mere Christianity* (New York: Touchstone, 1996), 176.

Chapter 6

Possessed by Promises

Meditating on the promises of God will strengthen you.

Throughout this book I have been showing how the tools we use to strengthen ourselves in the Lord are designed to keep us connected with our identity and purpose. Perhaps this is obvious, but we only know our identity and purpose because God *tells* us what they are. Renewing our minds requires us to learn how to let His words over our lives completely cancel out our old beliefs about who we are—even before we see His word manifesting fully in us. This is how we demonstrate faith.

David's destiny to be king did not begin with his ascent to the throne but with God's declaration of that destiny through the prophet Samuel. There were probably days in the wilderness when the only evidence he could present as proof that the Word was true was his memory of what Samuel said and the oil dripping from his head. But the fact that David pursued his destiny to its fulfillment, without quitting and without taking shortcuts, is clear evidence that he believed what God had said. His faith was not based on circumstances, but on who he knew God to be from his history with Him. Like Sarah, he "*judged Him faithful who had promised*" (Heb. 11:11).

Unlocking the Potential of the Promise

When you are born again, you inherit every promise of God for the believer. Peter tells us that these "*great and precious promises*" are the things that make us "*partakers of the divine nature*" (see 2 Peter 1:4)—they unlock our potential to become like Christ. But we don't truly possess these promises until three things happen. We first begin to possess a promise when it is spoken into our hearts by the Holy Spirit. As we read in the previous chapter, the Holy Spirit takes what is Christ's and declares it to us, telling us things to come (see John 16:13-14). The declaration of the Spirit is what places the promises of the Kingdom into our account. Whenever God speaks to us, His prophetic anointing is released in what He says. That word may come to you through another person, or an anointed prayer that is being prayed over you, a passage of Scripture that leapt out at you as you read, a dream or vision, or by the still, small voice of the Spirit in your inner man. That anointing does not just tell you what will be; it is *creating* what will be. It's as if a railroad track is being laid down before you that leads directly to the fulfillment of the Word.

It is impossible for God to lie. His Word is always in complete agreement with His nature and character, and therefore His very words release His power to accomplish what He has said. This is what the angel declared to Mary: "*For with God nothing will be impossible*" (Luke 1:37). The word for "word" is *rhema*, which is the freshly spoken Word of God. The word "impossible" means without ability. An expanded literal translation of this verse could be, "No freshly spoken word from God will ever come to you that does not contain its own ability to perform itself!"

This latent power in the promises of God increases our understanding of why we can trust the faithfulness of the One who promises. And a practical demonstration of trust is precisely the next thing that needs to happen for you to possess your promises. Thankfully, you don't need to understand the Word in order to show the Lord that you trust His Word as truth. You start moving down that railroad track to your destiny by simply *receiving* the Word. That's what Mary did after hearing the amazing promise that she would bear the Christ-child. She responded to the angel, "*Let it be to me according to your Word*" (Luke 1:38). There was no way she could comprehend what the angel had said to her or see how it could possibly happen. All she needed to know was that the Lord had spoken and that she could trust Him. As a result of her faith, she will be called "blessed" for eternity. What a destiny!

The third thing that must happen for you to possess your promises is that your faith in the promise must be tested and proven. Paul gave this instruction to Timothy: "*This charge I commit to you, son Timothy, according to the prophecies made concerning you, that by them you may wage a good warfare*" (1 Tim. 1:18). When the Holy Spirit declares a promise into your account, He has also put a weapon into your arsenal. This tells us two things. First, you will often have to contend for that Word against someone who will try to steal it from you. Secondly, if you contend for the promise by using the promise, you will be victorious. We can see this in the life of Christ. At His baptism, the Father made a declaration over him—"*This is my beloved Son in whom I am well pleased.*" Then Jesus was led into the desert to be tempted by the devil, who said, "If you are the Son of God...." The enemy was directly challenging the Word God had spoken. Jesus replied with Scripture: "*Man...*[lives] *by every word that proceeds from the mouth of God*" (Matt. 4:4). He stood on the promise of the Father on the basis of the fact that God was the One who had made the promise, and God's Words are the source of life. He refused to engage in pointlessly trying to determine His life outside of that Word. He had enough proof that the Father's Word over His life was true, not because He could point to evidence of its manifestation, but because He had *heard* the Word and *received* it.

Positioned for Fulfillment

Jesus' response teaches us that the only way we can position ourselves to see our promises fulfilled is by refusing to define ourselves according to anything but what God has said about us. Jesus rebuked the Pharisees in Mark 7:13, for "*making the Word of God of no effect through your tradition which you have handed down....*" In other words, the Pharisees insisted on defining themselves and their world according to human interpretation and practice rather than the Word of God. The words "of no effect" mean to *render powerless,* giving the picture of pulling the plug on the most powerful thing in the universe—the Word of God. Nothing can diminish the fact that His Word comes fully equipped. But we can shut off our access to that power by choosing to define our lives outside of what God has said.

Defining ourselves by the Word of God requires that we constantly train our minds to think in agreement with that Word. This means we have to remind ourselves of His promises often. But don't stop there! Learn to *meditate* on them. Like Mary, we must treasure them up and ponder them in our hearts (see Luke 2:19). While Eastern meditation tries to get people to empty their minds, biblical meditation focuses on our filling our minds—and our mouths—with the truth. Joshua 1:8 says, "*This Book of the Law shall not depart from your* ***mouth****, but you shall meditate in it day and night, that you may observe to do according to all that is written in it. For then you will make your way prosperous, and then you will have good success.*" One of the definitions for the Hebrew word "meditate" is "to mutter." Meditating involves repeating the words God has said *out loud.* As

Joshua was told, this regular repetition of what God had said is the key to our ability to *do* the Word. When we declare the Word over our own life and prophesy our own destiny in agreement with Him, we release the anointing of the Spirit in a greater measure to bring the Word to pass. The verse says that when we do this, we are actually *making* our way prosperous. Meditating on the promises of God is something we can do and are responsible to do in order to determine where we're going in life; it is a vital tool for strengthening ourselves in the Lord so we can walk in our identity and purpose. Meditating on the promises of God will strengthen you.

Meditating on the promises of God will strengthen you.

Manning the Rudder of My Ship

I write down the promises and prophecies that are spoken over me. Like the rudder of a ship, they determine the direction for my thoughts and desires, and eventually my life. I put the shorter ones on 3x5 cards, and the longer ones I keep in a file on my computer. They are in my briefcase and go wherever I go—and I read them often. Since I spend about half the year on the road, I take them with me so I can meditate on them while I'm flying. I often look around and see various businessmen and women who represent companies

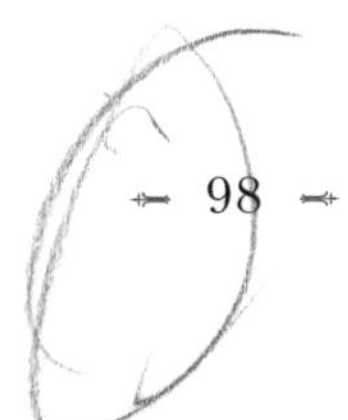

like Apple Computer or Ford Motor Company. Usually they are looking over their business plans and the notes for their strategic meetings. I, in turn, am examining the mind of Christ about me. Those little 3x5 cards remind me that I represent the Kingdom of God, and that my mind and body must stay current with my role and responsibilities as a delegated authority in this world. I can't afford to have thoughts in my head about me that God doesn't have in His. It's impossible to be consistently effective in fulfilling His purposes unless I am continually training my mind to think of myself according to what God says about me.

I also regularly read portions of Scripture that have been quickened in my heart by the Holy Spirit as words for my life. He has given me personal ownership of the promises through His declaration. I liken these promises as rooms in a mansion that are specifically designed for me; they are realms in God that are great *abiding places.* Romans 8:23 says that we "*groan within ourselves*" in our desire to see our destiny fulfilled. I believe that this is what the psalmist describes when he says, "*Deep calls unto deep*" (Psalm 42:7). The deep cry of my heart calls to the deep desire of the Lord to see me fulfill my potential as His son—the potential that is prophesied in these portions of Scriptures that He has declared over me. If I'm feeling heavy or discouraged, I'll read these passages until I sense the reality of that dwelling place, and can feel that promise burning in my heart once again. Joshua 1:5-9 has been one of my "rooms" for 35 years. It's not just a verse I've memorized;

it's the Word of the Lord for my life, so I go there often and find rest and refreshing, and I renew my perspective on my divine purpose.

But perhaps the most important part of this practice has to do with my experience in the book of Psalms. If I am being bombarded mentally or emotionally, or am just spiritually drained and struggling with my faith, I go to the Psalms. I read and continue to read until I *hear my voice.* Every human condition known to mankind is found in those songs: and I know there will be something there that will address my situation. There are times when I've read 20 or more psalms before finding my heart's cry on the pages of that Book. And when I do, I know I have found a resting place. I stay there and feed my soul by reading it over and over again. Sometimes I'll sing the words to a spontaneous melody. Other times, I use the things discussed in the psalm like "weapons" in praise—except I'm not focused on the devil. I use this "abiding place" to "faith my way" out of any hole I find myself in.

Inheriting Promises

It's so important to "treasure up and ponder" the promises of the Lord over your life. Your demonstrated value for the voice of the Lord is what determines the degree to which you attract more promises into your life. Romans 10:17 says that "*faith comes by hearing.*" And Hebrews 11:33 says that it was through faith that the saints of old "*obtained promises.*" The link between "hearing" and "obtaining promises" is faith. When we treasure His promises by holding them close to our heart and anchoring our soul in them through prayerful meditation, we are demonstrating that we believe they are true, and we are showing practical trust in the One who has given them to us. That trust shows Him that He can trust us with more.

The fact that the Holy Spirit is assigned to us to transfer our inherited promises into our account makes it clear that we need to have an ongoing relationship of hearing Him. Life does not come from every word that has already been spoken, but by every word that "***proceeds** from the mouth of God*" (Matt. 4:4). Notice "proceeds" is present tense. It is the Holy Spirit's breath on the pages of Scripture that brings us into the place of life and purpose. When we take what we hear and meditate on it, allowing it to train our thinking, our affections, and our behavior, it becomes an abiding word in us. The abiding Word creates a reality in our lives that resonates with the voice of the Spirit, enabling us to perceive it when it comes. Jesus rebuked the Pharisees on this point:

> *And the Father Himself, who sent Me, has testified of Me. You have neither heard His voice at any time, nor seen His form. But you do not have His Word abiding in you, because whom He sent, Him you do not believe. You search the Scriptures, for in them you think you have eternal life; and these are they which testify of Me. But you are not willing to come to Me that you may have life* (John 5:37-40).

In other words, the sign that the Word is abiding in you is that you recognize the presence of God and have faith for what He wants to do! His rebuke also implies that the Scriptures can only help in establishing that abiding Word in us if we respond to them by turning to the *Person* of Christ for life. Revelation is to bring us into a divine encounter, or else it will only make us religious (satisfied with form without power.) When we've been given a promise from the Scripture, it should provoke us to seek the One who both gives and fulfills His Word. On the other hand, when we don't have His Word abiding in us, the implication is serious. The Pharisees made the greatest error of all. They prayed the prayers for the Messiah to come, but never recognized Him for who He was, even when He was right in front of them. It was all because the Word was not abiding in them, as stated in John 5:38, "*But you do not have His Word abiding in you, because whom He sent, Him you do not believe.*"

We live by every word that proceeds from His mouth. Likewise, when we fail to listen to and live by that Word, we cut ourselves off from life. With stakes so high, I would strongly urge you to collect and record the prophetic words and promises over your life. Take a risk! Even write down the ones you're not sure of, and see if God will breathe on them in such a way that they become life to you. And equally important, review them often.

I would also urge you to read the Scriptures from the posture of "leaning into His voice." Expectation has everything to do with what you receive from God. Rather than expecting to gain mere information, answers to your questions, or "proof texts" to make a point, listen for the voice of the Spirit to take the words on the page and deposit them into your heart as a personal word for *you.* When you hear it, it will create that distinctive resonating in your spirit that makes you say, "Wow! I really have no idea what that means yet, but that's so right!" Receive it, write it down, meditate on it, declare it over your life, and let it draw you down the track into your eternal purpose.

Chapter 7

Keeping the Testimony

Testimonies of God connect generations to His promises.

As kings and priests of the planet, we have a dual responsibility: first to act as representatives of man to God through intercession, and secondly to act as representatives of God to man by proclaiming and demonstrating the Gospel of the Kingdom. Christ is our model in both of these roles. In His death, He represented sinful humanity to God and took our judgment. Now, "...*He always lives to make intercession for* [us]" (Heb. 7:25). And as a representative from God to man, Colossians tells us that Christ is "*the image of the invisible God*" and that "*it pleased the Father that in Him all the fullness should dwell*" (Col. 1:15,19). That means that Jesus is perfect theology. If we are tempted to believe something about God that we can't see revealed in Christ, then we'd better reject it. In His life and ministry, Jesus perfectly *re-presented* the Father by doing what His Father did and saying what His Father said.

One of the primary truths that Jesus proved is that it is simply impossible to represent God accurately without demonstrations of power. Miracles are not something that only Jesus and a small number of highly anointed ministers are expected to produce. The anointing that was on Christ is the same Holy Spirit who has been given to *every* believer. He is the One who qualifies us as members of the royal priesthood of God and calls us to continue the ministry of Christ by demonstrating what God is like through the miraculous.

TESTIMONIES REVEAL GOD'S NATURE

A doctrine of demons has been at work for many years to deny the people of God legal access to the realm of the miraculous as an essential element of their identity and purpose as believers. Thankfully, this revelation is currently being restored on a widespread basis. With it comes the revelation of one of the most profound treasures and tools we have inherited—the testimony. A testimony is the written or spoken record of anything that God has done, and every part of that record becomes your family history the moment you are born again. David declared "*I have inherited Your testimonies forever, for they are the joy of my heart*" (Ps. 119:111 NASB). This means that every story of every miracle or sign that God has ever performed is your story because you have become related to the God who made them happen.

The testimonies of God are the tools that equip us to walk in our purpose to demonstrate what He is like through the miraculous. First, they reveal the nature of God and how He does things—His ways. Secondly, this awareness of who God is creates an expectation in our hearts for God's ways to be manifested in our lives. The Hebrew root word for "testimony" means "do again." Every record of what God has done in generations past is a promise of what He will do again in our lives, because He is the same yesterday, today and forever, and is no respecter of persons (see Heb. 13:8; Acts 10:34). Not only that, Revelation 19:10 says, "*the testimony of Jesus is the spirit of prophecy.*" As you read in the previous chapter, the prophetic anointing does not just declare what God wants do to, but also carries creative power to bring what is declared into being. The testimony releases this anointing. When we declare what God has done, power is released to make that testimony happen again in the lives of those who hear it.

The testimonies of God are what connect each succeeding generation of believers to His covenant promises. For this reason, God put specific instructions in the Law of Moses for the people of Israel to rehearse the testimony on a daily basis and teach it to their children. Their entire social and family life was to be built on the repetition of the testimony (see Deut. 6). They also had to build memorial stones, such as the ones they were commanded to set up after crossing the Jordan River into the Promised Land, representing what God had done. Testimonies of God connect generations to His promises. When the children of the next generation passed by these stones and asked about them, their parents were to give the testimony (see Joshua 4:5-7) of that crossing, with the implication that, "This is your God too! You inherit this land and the promises that He gave us, and He is ready to keep those promises in your generation." David explains it like this:

Testimonies of God connect generations to His promises.

> *For He established a testimony in Jacob, And appointed a law in Israel, Which He commanded our fathers, That they should make them known to their children; That the generation to come might know them, The children who would be born, That they may arise and declare them to their children, That they may set their hope in God, And not forget the works of God, But keep His commandments* (Psalm 78:5-7).

Creating Expectation

Keeping the testimony caused Israel to "set their hope in God"—that is, to sustain their expectation for God to keep His promises through His miraculous invasions of power. Our expectation of God is what determines our level of faith. And we have to have faith in order to "keep His commandments." All of Christ's commands, from "heal the sick" to "love your neighbor" are only possible to fulfill through the supernatural empowerment of His Spirit that comes through faith. Likewise, the Israelites were given a mission from God to take the Promised Land from their enemies and establish themselves as a nation, a mission that entirely depended on their ability to position themselves for the invasion of God's power through faith. He was the one who gave them the strategies and the strength to do the impossible. As long as they remembered what God had said and done and stepped out in faith with His strategies, they won supernatural victories. But when the people stopped keeping the testimony, their faith for the miraculous diminished, and so did their obedience to His commands. If you study the history of Israel in the Old Testament, you'll find that every generation that stopped walking in their covenant with God did so because they forgot His works. David goes on in Psalm 78 to describe such a generation:

> *The children of Ephraim, being armed and carrying bows, Turned back in the day of battle. They did not keep the covenant of God, They refused to walk in His law, And forgot His works And His wonders that He had shown them* (Psalm 78:9-11).

You'll notice that these people were equipped for battle: *being armed and carrying bows.* The problem was not that God had sent them into battle without preparation.

They possessed the testimonies of what God had done for their fathers that, if declared, would not only give them the courage to step out in faith but would release a prophetic anointing to repeat those acts. The problem was that they had forgotten them. Thus they lacked the strength and faith needed to face the battle.

The Cost of Neglect

I'm amazed at the human capacity to forget the most extraordinary, mind-boggling things, particularly the miraculous—but it usually doesn't happen overnight. Forgetting is a downward spiral that begins with the very natural tendency to gradually talk less about the cancer that was instantly healed, for example. Other things start to occupy our minds. But then, the less we keep the testimony in our conversation and our minds, the lower goes our expectation to see the miraculous. Our lowered expectation keeps us from recognizing and stepping into opportunities to see the miraculous. And the less we experience the miraculous, the less we have to talk about. We talk less, expect less, and experience less until we end up in the place where we meet someone with cancer and we go, "God! Help!" Our expectation and faith are small, even though we've seen God fix this problem before. We are armed and carrying bows, but we've forgotten that fact; and unless we remember what God has done and rise up in the faith provided in the testimony, we will turn back from the divine opportunities for victory right in front of us.

If you've studied the Old Testament, you know that the failure of Israel to keep the testimony and defeat the enemies in their land had serious consequences. By choosing instead to coexist with their enemies in the same territory, they became vulnerable to idolatry, which led them to break their covenant with God and invite all kinds of curses and problems into their lives. They lost their identity as the people of God and became just like the people around them. Failing to keep the testimony not only makes us forget who God is, but who we are. Like Israel, the only thing that distinguishes believers from the rest of the world is the reality that God is active among us. When we lose sight of that, we are no different than anyone else—with one exception, we will experience more serious consequences because we are accountable for the revelation of God we've received in the testimonies. We rob people of their encounters with Him when we forget that the testimony matters to God.

KEEPING AWARE OF THE GOD WHO INVADES THE IMPOSSIBLE

What does it take to keep the testimony so we can stay out of the downward spiral and carry out our responsibility to represent God with power? It simply takes following the prescriptions that God gave His people in the first place. We are to establish a culture of the testimony in our personal lives, in our homes, and in our churches. We're to talk about it when we get up, when we eat a meal, when we go to work, and when we go to bed. We're to build memorials that remind us of what God has done and consider them regularly.

I started keeping a journal a number of years ago for the sole purpose of recording the miracles I've witnessed. I'm not the best at journaling, but I am deeply convinced of the power I've seen and my own human ability to forget what I've witnessed. I believe in the weightiness of the consequences if I should forget His miracles, so I journal. I owe my children, grandchildren, and future generations a record of the interventions of God in my generation. The testimony itself is their inheritance.

As a pastor, I have emphasized this principle to my staff and our congregation. Our team begins every staff and board meeting with an hour or two of sharing testimonies of what God has done in the previous weeks and months. We know that we can't afford to make plans for the direction of the church without an overwhelming awareness of the God who invades the impossible. If we lack that awareness, we will lack faith and courage, and our plans will fall short of the mission God has given us. When we have that awareness, however, we not only leave our meetings feeling incredibly encouraged by the goodness and power of God, we leave full of faith that God intends to do it all again this week. We also walk out carrying a full arsenal of testimonies that contain the potential to multiply themselves as we declare them over the lives of people we have the opportunity to touch.

If I don't stay aware of the God who invades the impossible, I will reduce ministry to my ministry gifts. All of our gifts are like the sails on a boat. We can sit in the harbor (church) and admire one another's sails; but without wind they are worthless! Our gifts are designed to catch the wind of God so we can accomplish what is humanly impossible. The testimony keeps our sails hoisted.

As for our congregation and our School of Ministry, they have equally embraced the value of the testimony. Many of the testimonies we share at our staff and board meetings are their stories, which means that the people are not just out there ministering in the power of God, they're talking about it and it's getting back to us. One of the most significant fruits of this testimony culture is that more and more of the stories we're hearing are related to the sharing of testimonies.

One Sunday when I taught on the power of the testimony, we showed a video in our service of a little boy running around after his club feet had been healed. After seeing this video, some students from the School of Ministry were so excited that they went down to the mall the next day to pray for anyone they could find. They saw a woman walking with a leg brace and a cane, so they naturally assumed she was a target for a miracle. They began talking to her and shared the testimony about the boy whose feet had been healed. Moved by the story, she allowed them to pray for her knee, which had a tumor on it. The tumor disappeared, so she took off her brace. Then one of the young men who was praying for her said, "The fire of God is hitting your back right here," and pointed to a particular spot. In surprise she felt the spot and found that another tumor, which she had kept to herself, had also disappeared! She walked out of the mall carrying her brace and cane on one arm, and her grandchild on the other, to whom the students heard her explain, "I don't need these anymore."

This woman experienced the prophetic power of the testimony. Declaring the testimony created a divine moment for God to do it again! And the miracles that occur when testimonies are shared continue to multiply—not only in our community, but all over the world. There is perhaps no other revelation that I've seen so dramatically change how people "do church" in the places where I travel and teach than the power of the testimony because it is calling them back to their true identity and purpose in God.

Leaving an Inheritance Through Testimony

Keeping the testimony is a responsibility that God gave to every man and woman in Israel, not merely their leaders. The fact that each individual is accountable for keeping the testimony as a lifestyle defines this as one of the primary tools we must use to strengthen ourselves. We can't expect others to keep the testimony for us. Beyond keeping testimonies in our conversation, we are also to meditate on them. Meditation is powerful because it involves our imagination, which actually can lead us into a significant level of experience, and experience is a vital part of renewing the mind. The writer of Psalm 66 says, "*Come and see the works of God...He turned the sea into dry land; they went through the river on foot.*" This writer could not have possibly seen God part the Red Sea and the Jordan River. But through inspired imagination, he was able to come into a level of experiencing these miracles that enabled him to own these events as his own history. If you are someone who feels like you haven't seen very many miracles, you first need to remember that you possess every story of God's as your own. Then, because they're yours, you should study the testimonies of Scripture and collect the testimonies of both historical saints and the saints around you so you can meditate on them. Meditation on the testimonies trains your mind to think from the realm of faith.

David made it clear that it was his study of the testimonies that enabled him to access such a powerful revelation of God: "*I have more understanding than all my teachers, for Your testimonies are my meditation*" (Ps. 119:99). And because of his level of revelation, David became the only man in the Old Testament to walk the dual role of king and priest. If the testimonies brought David into that destiny before he could experience unbroken communion with God through the

Holy Spirit, how much more will they bring us into our destiny now that we have the Spirit of Revelation within us? As kings and priests, our entire identity stands on the foundation of our family history in God. If we don't know where we came from, we won't know where we're going or how to get there. We must learn to keep the testimony.

Chapter 8

CONTROLLING YOUR ENVIRONMENT

Jesus was moved to action,
not by human need,
but by His Father's heart.

As I have developed a lifestyle of feeding on the promises and prophecies of God over my life and meditating on His testimonies, something interesting has happened. People with testimonies now constantly find me, like heat-seeking missiles. Because the nature of the testimony carries a prophetic anointing, it's as though I am prophesied over on a continual basis. As a result, I have a steady supply of encouragement and strength that shows up wherever I am, all over the world. It's amazing. When we value what God values, His blessings will hunt us down.

Jesus made a statement that explains how our value for the testimonies and promises of the Lord draws more of them into our lives. He said, "'*Take heed what you hear. With the same measure you use, it will be measured to you; and to you who hear, more will be given*'" (Mark 4:24). Clearly Jesus is not referring merely to the physical act of perceiving sound. He's talking about hearing that involves listening. When we listen, we allow what we are hearing to gain our attention and focus, which in turn influences our beliefs and values. These beliefs and values set a standard for our ears that ultimately determines the voices that we pick up in our environment. This standard is also what draws us to certain people more than others.

Because I've set a standard for my ears by valuing the testimony, I attract people with the same standard. On the other hand, people with an ungodly standard are attracted to people with that same standard. If we were to take someone with a reputation for loving gossip and put that person into a new job with 50 other employees they'd never met, within seven days every other gossip-lover in the place would be drawn to that person. Our values communicate something in the spiritual realm that alerts others with the same values to our presence.

Setting a Standard for Our Ears

The standard we set for our ears also determines our ability to strengthen ourselves because strengthening ourselves begins with our choice to listen to God's voice more than any other. By the way, I hope it's obvious that learning to strengthen ourselves does not imply that we are the source of our strength. Rather, "*I can do all things* ***through Christ*** *who strengthens me*" (Phil. 4:13). And Christ "[upholds] *all things by the word of His power"—including us* (Heb. 1:3). Thus, every tool in our arsenal is designed to help us draw from the strength made available to us by hearing His voice. Listening is what enables us to establish agreement with Him through obeying His voice, and our agreement is what releases heavenly strength and resources into our lives and circumstances. However, as I just described, the standard we set for our ears can attract heavenly strength that comes through interactions with other people who speak and live from a heavenly perspective. Therefore, by purposefully associating with people who share our values and controlling our interactions with people who don't, we strengthen ourselves.

I strongly believe that we are all called to minister to anyone and everyone to whom the Holy Spirit would lead us. We're to accept them unconditionally and show them the love and power of God. Certainly there will also be individuals who God calls us to do business with, to befriend over a period of time in order to introduce them to Jesus, or to disciple in the faith. But these kinds of relationships are a completely different ballgame from friendships in which we open ourselves to the influence of our friend's perspective and values. We need to be careful about who is close to us and gives input into our lives.

STRENGTH COMES FROM COVENANT PEOPLE

Our close friendships, especially with our spouses, are powerful, because they are built on covenant.

Covenant establishes an agreement that allows the spiritual reality that governs your life to flow to the other person, and vice versa. This is why it is so vital to develop friendships with people whose lives consistently display the fruit of the Kingdom. When we steward covenant friendships with people of faith, we stay connected to a growing source of strength that often greatly determines our ability to persevere through difficult times.

I am blessed to have close friendships with people of genuine faith. Time and time again I have been uplifted and strengthened simply by being with them. Often I was not even able to mention the difficult situation I was facing at the time, yet I left encouraged. There are several reasons for this. First, our love and honor for one another creates an exchange of life whenever we interact. Because my friends are people of faith, they naturally exude hope, promise, and joy. It doesn't take long when I'm with them for their attitude and spirit to be infectious. But even more, covenant friendships, when they're built on knowing each other after the Spirit, have the effect of calling us back to who we truly are in Christ. They refresh our connection to our purpose and identity, and when our vision for those things is renewed, usually our strength is too. For this reason, I know that one of the best ways to strengthen myself when I'm tired or discouraged is to grab hold of a friend and spend some time with him.

Keep the Weeds Out of the Garden

On the other hand, I have found that when I am in an emotionally vulnerable place, or even if I'm just physically tired, I have to be careful to make sure I am not around people who like to complain or be critical. I have always had strong personal boundaries in place for discerning and interacting with people who speak from a place of negativity or unbelief. Normally I will minister to them, but I will not give them access to my life. When I'm lacking strength, however, I will intentionally avoid them. It may not sound very compassionate, but I am the only one who is responsible for keeping my heart free from doubt and judgment, and I alone can recognize when I am vulnerable to the influence of people who agree with those spirits. The powerful effect of people's personalities and values are given as a warning by Solomon when he says, "*Do not associate with a man given to anger; or go with a hot-tempered man, or you will learn his ways and find a snare for yourself*" (Prov. 22:24-25 NASB).

Not all ungodly counsel comes from the ungodly. While many mean well, they lack the faith perspective that I strive for, and tend to work to make me more like them than they do to actually try to help me to become stronger in my trust in God. My job is to protect myself from such an influence, especially when I am vulnerable. My heart is a garden. Some people are good at planting weeds, while others plant the Kingdom. My job, and yours, is to know the difference.

The Place of Solitude

The gospels specifically mention occasions in which Jesus took His disciples away from the crowds to rest and be together. The testimony of revival history teaches us that very few men and women of God really learn how and when to do this. In case after case, the same person who carried a marvelous anointing that brought salvation, healing, and deliverance to thousands of people lacked the wisdom to see that he wouldn't be able to sustain that ministry if he didn't learn to get away from the crowds long enough to get physical rest and cultivate life-giving relationships with family and friends who would reaffirm his or her focus on the Kingdom. As a result, many of these revivalists died young, and many of their family members suffered physically and spiritually.

We can't afford to miss the lesson these stories teach us. If we are going to become people who God can entrust with greater measures of favor and anointing to fulfill our purpose as a royal priesthood, we have to be people who are prepared for the reality that we are going to attract needy people. People's needs can exert tremendous pressure on us, and that pressure will expose the places in our heart that care more about meeting the expectations of others than doing only what Jesus is doing. In His ministry, Jesus met the needs of many people, but He also walked past a lot of other needy people. He understood that as one man, the only way He could succeed at what He was doing was to keep Himself in a place where what moved Him to action was not merely human need, but the actual heart of His Father. Jesus was moved to action not by human need but by His Father's heart.

Jesus was moved to action not by by human need but by His Father's heart.

The strength of our intimacy with the Father and with the close covenant relationships in our lives is what will largely determine our ability to minister from a place of faith and obedience to God rather than a place of striving to please or help people. The people who are most vulnerable to overextending themselves on behalf of ministry relationships are people who struggle with intimacy—both with God and others. Ministry can be a great place for them to feel connected and loved, but the truth is, without the accountability that only comes from covenant friendships, they are just being set up for burnout or compromise. This is why God will pull many ministers out of ministry for a time just to learn how to be friends with Him apart from working for Him. All true fruitfulness flows from that intimacy with Him.

I have found that there are three main sources of distractions that we must learn to overcome in order to stay on track with our destiny.

First, there are the distractions from the devil. He plays on our old fears and addictions to get us to sin.

Gradually, as our minds are transformed and our senses are trained to hunger and thirst for God, those temptations don't really hold much interest anymore.

Secondly, in that transformation process, we deal more with distractions from ourselves—places where our old, limited ways of thinking keep us from perceiving and responding to what God is trying to teach us.

But in the end, some of the most difficult distractions to avoid are not the ones that come from the devil or ourselves. They're from God. They're the blessings, the favor, the prosperity, the miracles, and all the amazing gifts that He pours out in our lives. Obviously He gave them to us for our enjoyment and success. But they also have a way of revealing whether we will choose the benefits of friendship above the Friend Himself.

Every time we start to coast on the benefits of our covenant relationships with God and those closest to us, we are going to violate love. It must be settled in our hearts that we maintain a posture of intentionally pursuing these relationships for their own sakes, and for what we can bring to them. We also have to purpose never to let the needs of people we are not in covenant with dictate what we have to give to our close relationships. In our commitment to use the strength we have for their blessing, we actually sow into the moment when we will need strength for ourselves. That's the nature of our Father's Kingdom.

Healthy Humor

One final note: most of the people of faith who consistently make a contribution to my life in times of need are also people with a great sense of humor. I tend to take myself too seriously and resist laughter in difficult times. Joy in trial takes faith; but being with people I trust enough to relax around helps to foster the atmosphere where laughter comes easily and often. Sometimes just being together, telling funny stories, sharing joyful experiences, and even laughing at myself, is just what the doctor ordered. Laughter really is good medicine.

Chapter 9

The Desperate Cry

Focus on God's answers—
not your problems.

God wants us to succeed!

The Holy Spirit will give
you water to sustain you through
the dry and barren times.

The tools presented in this book are not meant to be an exhaustive list of the ways we can strengthen ourselves in the Lord. I have only addressed the things with which I have the most experience. My goal is to convince you that God has equipped you with everything you need to fulfill your destiny. It's not complicated. What is most important to me is for the Body of Christ to be *absolutely possessed* by the revelation of the greatness of our destiny. Without this understanding, we will probably not be willing to pay the price of learning to strengthen ourselves.

SURPRISED BY JOY

The Holy Spirit is the only One who can reveal who we're called to be. This is why the conviction of the Holy Spirit is one of the most precious gifts we receive throughout our lifetimes. Sadly, for years this gift has been confused with its very antithesis: the condemnation of the enemy. One of the clearest pictures of the difference between conviction and condemnation is found in the Book of Nehemiah. As you may know, Nehemiah led the Jewish exiles in the task of rebuilding the walls of Jerusalem and restoring the city following their Babylonian captivity. At one point the people set aside a day to renew their covenant with God by listening to the elders read and explain the Book of the Law, which they had not heard for years. As they understood the words that were read, they saw how high God's standard for their lives was and how far below it they actually lived. They naturally started weeping and mourning. But Nehemiah and the other leaders corrected them for this response to the Holy Spirit's conviction:

> *And Nehemiah, who was the governor, Ezra the priest and scribe, and the Levites who taught the people said to all the people, "This day is holy to the Lord your God; do not mourn nor weep." For all the people wept, when they heard the words of the Law.*
>
> *Then he said to them, "Go your way, eat the fat, drink the sweet, and send portions to those for whom nothing is prepared; for this day is holy to our Lord. Do not sorrow, for the joy of the Lord is your strength."*
>
> *So the Levites quieted all the people, saying, "Be still, for the day is holy; do not be grieved." And all the people went their way to eat and drink, to send portions and rejoice greatly, because they understood*

the words that were declared to them (Nehemiah 8:9-12)

For many who were raised in church, weeping over the fact that we don't measure up to God's standard for life as taught in the Scriptures is considered the one *legitimate* sign of conviction and repentance. And *holiness* is something generally associated with somberness and tears and not with joy. That *bent* in our value system has caused us to mislabel many things in life, such as the frequent mistake of referring to depressed individuals as "prophets" or at least as "intercessors." But in Nehemiah's story of rebuilding the fallen city of Jerusalem, we discover that holiness is more connected to joy and rejoicing. Israel was forbidden to weep when the priest publicly read God's Word, even though they fell far short of what God required from them. They were given a warning not to weep, and instead rejoice and celebrate with a feast. Absolutely shocking! Sinners were to celebrate with joy because they *understood* God's call to holiness!

The idea that the best response to conviction is getting depressed derives from wrong beliefs that blind us to the Holy Spirit's purpose in exposing the places where we fall short of our high calling in Christ. There is a place for tears in this process as we're told that it is godly sorrow that leads us to repentance. But when we have a wrong view of God as a legalistic father who is unhappy with our every move, we distort what was supposed to lead us to an encounter with Him that brings transformation. Instead, many develop attitudes of somberness in a fleshly attempt to be holy. Consequently, we've misunderstood and misappropriated the fullness of His grace, which does not merely forgive our sin, but empowers us to live like Him. These beliefs create an opportunity for the *accuser of the brethren* to speak up in the moments when we see areas of sin or weakness in our lives, and convince us that we're hopeless cases. We are deceived into thinking that his accusations are godly conviction because we can't deny the fact that we need to change.

The Needed Shift in Focus

The real problem is not in what we lack, but how we respond to what God has said. Focusing on our problems more than God's answers should be a dead giveaway that we're really dealing with condemnation, not the Holy Spirit's conviction. Focus on God's answers—not your problems. When the Holy Spirit shows us where we are falling short, the bigger reality is not the areas where we're not yet walking in our destiny, but the destiny itself. So many of us read the verse that "*all have sinned and fall short of the glory of God*" (Rom. 3:23) and focus more on the fact that all have fallen short than the fact that we are destined for glory! The conviction

Focus on God's answers—not your problems.

of the Holy Spirit is actually a call to turn our focus away from our sin and our limitations. He's saying, "You're made for more than this. Lift your head and set your sights higher." Such a renewed perspective is supposed to seem overwhelmingly impossible. That way we're more likely to draw near to Him and allow His grace to bring us into our destiny.

When we recognize the purpose for the Holy Spirit's conviction, we start to understand how we need to interpret the kinds of tests He allows us to face in our lives. It's obvious that the real tests are not the situations that challenge our strengths, but the ones that expose our weaknesses. David's biggest test was not facing Goliath; it was overcoming his own vulnerability to distress by strengthening himself. In fact, most of the warfare we deal with in the Christian life is really internal. As we realign our wrong thinking and transform our old behavior patterns, it is amazing how we find that the devil and the world pose less and less of a threat to the flow of the life of God through us.

But, as previously mentioned, the thing we forget is that God prepares us for *all* of our battles. We have to remember that when our weaknesses are exposed, it is because God has already given us the tools we need to overcome them. This is why the Israelites were commanded to rejoice in the face of their shortcomings. The Holy Spirit not only convicted them of their destiny; He equipped them with a promise: "*The joy of the Lord is your strength.*" In other words, it's the Lord's joy over our lives that contains the strength needed to step toward our destiny. And how do we get that joy? We rejoice. We align our bodies and souls with the promise because that posture is what invites the manifestation of the promise. That this response to conviction is what God is looking for should make sense because it requires faith. To rejoice when you win the *Reader's Digest* Sweepstakes is easy, but to rejoice before you get your desired breakthrough takes faith.

Positioned to Receive

Receiving the promises of our destiny, as mentioned in Chapter 6, requires that we position ourselves in a certain way. Jesus gave His disciples a command: "*Behold, I send the Promise of My Father upon you; but tarry in the city of Jerusalem until you are endued with power from on high*" (Luke 24:49). I want to point out that this promise was not about their salvation. Jesus had already breathed on them and said, "...*Receive the Holy Spirit*" (John 20:22). He did this in direct parallel to the Father's first breathing life into Adam. It was an act of creation that fulfilled the promise of Psalm 102:18, that "...*a people yet to be created* [would] *praise the Lord.*" Since the salvation encounter is specifically what brings this new creation reality into our lives, I believe that this moment was when the disciples were born again. Pentecost was another event, a second touch. If their salvation had brought them *out of the red,* so to speak, Pentecost was about getting them into the black so they could minister in power more consistently and have something to give away to others.

So what had to happen between salvation and Pentecost? "*These all continued with one accord in prayer and supplication...*" (Acts 1:14). The word *continued* means "to be steadfastly attentive to; to persevere and not to faint; to be in constant readiness for." The disciples didn't assume the promise Jesus gave them would just happen, nor did they assume that "*tarrying in Jerusalem*" meant hanging out and doing business as usual. They stayed in one place and contended in prayer. When Heaven invaded earth on the Day of Pentecost, it was because earth had invaded Heaven for ten days. Their contending in faith for the promise both prepared them to receive it and enabled them to draw it to them.

CREATED FOR GLORY

The disciples were strengthening themselves in that upper room. Strengthening ourselves in the Lord is all about being prepared to receive and steward the fulfillment of our promises. Think of "invading Heaven" in the physical sense. In order for an astronaut to venture beyond the earth's atmosphere, he must be covered in a pressurized suit that can resist the vacuum of outer space. Without it, his body would instantly explode. If you and I are going to touch the realm of God's *glory*—and the word "glory" literally means "weight"—we are going to have to exert some internal pressure in order to build enough strength to live in that atmosphere and be carriers of that glory on earth.

And to carry His glory is exactly what we are made to do—the Christian life is not only about getting saved so we go to Heaven when we die. Rather, it's about learning to live in Heaven's reality now so that we can co-labor with Christ to establish His Kingdom on earth. The reason the Church has "dumbed down" the Great Commission of discipling nations and seeing the knowledge of the glory of the Lord cover the earth has everything to do with our failure to pick up the baton of the early church by contending for the authentic ongoing baptism of the Holy Spirit. As the Book of Acts testifies, this baptism was never meant as a one-time event but as an ongoing series of encounters that enable us to walk in increasing levels of power, fulfilling the assignment Jesus gave to His Body. Please note that some of the same people mentioned in the upper room in Acts 2 are also in the outpouring in Acts 4:29-31.

The indwelling Spirit we receive at salvation is the Spirit of adoption who calls out "Abba Father," and gives us unbroken access to His heart. The revelation of His Kingdom and knowledge of His will that is to come to earth pours forth in these encounters. But as we truly come to know the Father and what He wants to do, we should be convinced that knowing is not enough. His whole plan centers on the unveiling of His sons and daughters, who will walk in the authority

Jesus received at His death and bring liberty to all of creation (see Rom. 8:19-21). For this reason, the Holy Spirit did not come only to dwell within us, but to rest upon us with the same Christ-anointing Jesus had in order to release Heaven's answers to earth's dilemmas. In other words, He came to manifest the Kingdom. This is the *ongoing* baptism we need.

I am so grateful that in the last century the Holy Spirit has brought much of the Body of Christ worldwide back to the pursuit and experience of this baptism. What baffles me is that there are so many believers who taste of this glorious anointing and stop short of undertaking a lifelong pursuit of more. Every man and woman I know who has been launched into a ministry of signs and wonders through his or her experience with the Holy Spirit understands that he/she must never stop contending for and experiencing further encounters. However, they also understand that their journey of contending is a journey of stewardship. Too many people in revival don't know how to steward what they received when they were baptized in the Holy Ghost, so they keep coming back to the same place, asking God to fill them again. This mind-set lacks a fundamental understanding of how God establishes His Kingdom.

HOW THE KINGDOM COMES

At one point, Jesus picked up on His disciples' misunderstanding of how the Kingdom would come. After witnessing thousands of miracles, and signs and wonders confirming His message that "*the kingdom of heaven is at hand*," the disciples expected that "*the kingdom of God would appear immediately*" (Luke 19:11). So Jesus told them a parable about a nobleman who left the country and entrusted his servants with various sums of money to invest while he was gone. When the nobleman returned, he had each person give an account of what he had done with what he was given. In response he gave each person authority over cities in his realm in direct correlation to his ability to invest and manage what he had been given to steward. For example, the one who managed to use ten units of money well and gain ten more, he made the governor over ten cities. He then condemned the servant who had hidden the money rather than investing it (Luke 19:12-27). This is how the Kingdom of God comes—not all at once, but little by little as the people of God steward the anointing they received in their last encounter. We can't take cities and nations for God because He already possesses them. That's why in the second Psalm it says to ask God for the nations, and He'll give them to us as our inheritance. Our job is to become ones to whom He can entrust His authority until entire cities and nations come under the righteous influence of those who serve well, carrying God's agenda. This kind of increase comes to those who are faithful with what they've been given.

So how do we steward what's been given to us? We use the tools we've been given to contend for the promises and desires that God has birthed in our hearts through the Holy Spirit. We also take other specific steps of faith and obedience in order to line up our thinking and behavior with what we've heard. If you have a longing to preach the Gospel, a first step might be preaching to yourself in the car. It may be a small beginning, but we can't despise it because faith says that it's not where you are, but where you're going that is important. And faith understands that spiritual release comes through physical obedience.

Faith must conquer our fear of failure if we are going to fully embrace a journey of transformation. As the lesson from Nehemiah teaches, our promises and desires are usually connected to the places where we need to grow in our character and in our capacity to think and live like God. If there were no power to change, it would be cruel for God to give us promises that we could never qualify to receive. But because the Spirit of the resurrected Christ lives in our bodies, His promises and desires are the keys to our breakthrough. We have to come to see the places of lack in our lives as the very places where God intends to bring us into our greatest victories—if we will take the risk to step out on our promises.

FROM DESPERATION TO FAITH

For years I was bothered by the fact that even though I preached that God was a God of miracles, I wasn't seeing the miraculous. I couldn't be satisfied with just having good theology because my experience denied what my theology said. I went from being bothered to being consumed with godly jealousy when I heard reports of healings breaking out in The Vineyard Movement through John Wimber and others. In the midst of this season, I received a prophetic word from my friend Mario Murillo saying that God was going to anoint me to walk in a ministry of healing and miracles. I took that word, wrote it down, and began to declare it over my life on a regular basis. Over ten years ago, the Lord began to fulfill His word, and I have consistently and increasingly seen the miraculous as I minister the Gospel.

Recently I had an opportunity to reconnect with Mario, and I pulled out the worn 3x5 card with his prophetic word on it. Knowing how I had contended for the word, he began to explain to me that I was like Hannah. Hannah wanted the very thing that her barrenness prevented her from having—a child. But instead of succumbing to bitterness and disappointment, she cried out to the Lord. Hers had to be a cry of faith, because in that cry, she developed a resolve to set apart her desire completely to the Lord. She was so consumed by her desire that she lost all consciousness about what others thought of her. Mario explained that the Lord used my barrenness in the realm of miracles to develop that same desperate cry in me that Hannah had—to the point where I didn't care if I was misunderstood. In contending for the promise, I strengthened my resolve to guard the anointing jealously when it was finally given, and use it completely for the Lord's purposes. This resolve is essential in becoming trustworthy to experience the fulfillment of the promise.

As Jesus' parable on the talents indicates, the length of time between the day in which we are entrusted with a "talent" and the day in which God calls us to account for our stewardship is undetermined. I didn't know how long I would need to keep praying and laying hands on people in expectation for my prophetic word to be fulfilled. But my heart was set on pilgrimage. There was no "plan B." Because I lived in pursuit of the promise, each day brought me closer to my breakthrough. The very fact that I had a promise from God guaranteed that there would be a day in which the Lord would assess what I had done and judge whether my stewardship of the promise had adequately prepared me to steward the realm of anointing spoken of in the promise.

If we don't set our hearts on the end goal, we will despise the day of small beginnings. We also won't be able to recognize how far we've come from those beginnings. We have to learn to sustain deep gratitude for what God has done in the past while keeping our eyes fixed on the possibilities that are ever before us until the Kingdom comes in its fullness. With this perspective, we also need to sustain the awareness that we've already received whatever will be necessary for the next phase of our journey. God wants us to succeed!

God wants us to succeed!

God has set us up to succeed. Yes, He commanded us to disciple the nations. It looks like an impossible task. But Jesus is the Desire of the Nations, and He dwells inside us. He lives in us to make it possible for us to succeed in the impossible assignment to disciple nations. Our job is learning to let Him out, and we only do that to the degree that we are like Him. This is why the desire to become like Him is the driving passion of the Christian life. When we truly see who He is and what He's done for us, when we've tasted His love and power, a desperate conviction is born in us—we simply cannot live any longer with the areas in our lives that are inconsistent with who Jesus is. This conviction must grip our hearts so completely that we resolve never to quit until we are completely conformed to His image. In becoming like Christ, we become the very thing the world longs for.

Personal Transformation—The Ultimate Ambition

To be transformed into His image is the passion that drives our priority to learn how to strengthen ourselves. No one else can fulfill my destiny for me. No one else can possess my promises. Complacency will not draw the baptism of the Holy Spirit into my life. There's something about exercising my will and faith to step beyond convenience that matters to God. On one occasion, Jesus saw that His disciples were struggling in the midst of a storm, so He walked out on the lake. But He didn't walk to them. The Bible says,

"*He...would have passed them by*" (Mark 6:48). The *cry* of His disciples is what turned Him their way. He was showing them that God is available to us—He is always within reach.

God has already pursued us with a love so totally overwhelming that it will take all of eternity to plumb its depths. But He protects the opportunities that we have to use our will to pursue Him. That's how faith works. If He says He will catch us, we jump because only when we jump, can He do what He promised. Only as we step out to do the supernatural things He has asked of us can we appropriate the supernatural power He's already given us to achieve these impossible tasks.

The Sons of Korah give us a wonderful description of how this process of maturing in strength and character takes place in our lives:

Blessed is the man whose strength is in You, whose heart is set on pilgrimage.

> *As they pass through the Valley of Baca, they make it a spring; the rain also covers it with pools. They go from strength to strength; each one appears before God in Zion* (Psalm 84:5-7).

Baca means "weeping." The Valley of Weeping is a prophetic picture of any difficulty in our lives, every kind of loss, crisis, need, or pain. Those whose strength is in the Lord and whose hearts are set on His pilgrimage—on running the race to the end and fulfilling the destiny God has given them—can take those places of disappointment and turn them into a spring.

When we refuse to let circumstances and areas of personal weakness determine our level of faith and passion, we will discover the secret of victory in every situation. Instead of being bound by the limitations set by our natural environment, we choose to lift up our heart's cry to the Lord in the dry and barren place and actually draw "water" to the surface that the Holy Spirit has already poured out in our lives. It's much like digging in dry and cracked soil until you find water. But this water is actually a spring of great refreshing. It lies just beneath the surface of our driest set of circumstances. Remember, Jesus promised that rivers of living water would flow from our hearts (see John 7:38). The Holy Spirit will give you water to sustain you through the dry and barren times.

The Holy Spirit will give you water to sustain you through the dry and barren times.

It is very important to believe this is true. For then we are conscious of the fact that we are NEVER far from water! And when we stir up the passion of our hearts for the promises of God in a place of weakness, we not only create a spring, we attract the outpouring of the Spirit that covers that place with pools—new realms of anointing. When we discover springs beneath our dry moments, we attract rain. Water attracts water. Correctly stewarding the Holy Spirit's work in our past (digging in dry places) attracts the water of outpouring (that which is to come). This is Kingdom stewardship: taking the barren areas of our lives, the places of unfulfilled dreams and great disappointment, and drawing the springs of life from our own hearts, knowing that the Holy Spirit lives within us and is never without life to give. He who has promised is faithful. Fulfilling the demands of this principle of stewardship is how we "*go from strength to strength,*" and ultimately reach our destination, appearing "*before God in Zion*"—a picture that not only speaks of going to Heaven when we die, but of becoming people who live from Heaven toward earth, right now.

MY VALLEY OF WEEPING

In 2003, while on a ministry trip to Brazil with Randy Clark and his Global Awakening team, I received the news that during a simple surgical procedure, the doctors discovered pancreatic cancer in my dad. I left Brazil early to be with him and join my family in the battle for his life.

My dad has always been the greatest encouragement in my life. But he was that way to most everyone who knew him. He was a true Barnabas—*a son of encouragement.* In addition to all the obvious reasons to want my dad to live, I knew that I needed his continual help in what God was doing here in Redding, California. I also wanted him to see the fruit of his own labor—he was the pastor who had set the original course of direction for our church well over 20 years before I became the pastor.

I felt moved to ask God to repeat Hezekiah's miracle for my dad. While facing death, Hezekiah cried out to God and was given an additional 15 years of life on earth. Since God is no respecter of persons, and is the same yesterday, today, and forever, it seemed like an appropriate prayer for this situation. Great numbers of people started praying the same prayer, asking for the additional years given to Hezekiah to be given to my dad. In fact, one woman whom I had never met told me that God had spoken the same "Hezekiah miracle" to her to give me as a promise for my dad; I received it gladly.

Ironically, cancer has been a prayer target of ours for quite a few years. Cancer has become the Goliath that taunts the armies of the living God and I have a righteous anger over the violation of the name of the Lord. We refuse to show any respect for the name cancer, as it is inferior to the name of Jesus. Through the years, we have seen a great number of cancer cases healed in and through our church. In fact, someone in our town actually started a rumor after their own healing: "Go to Bethel; they don't tolerate cancer!" While we have not seen everyone healed who comes to us, we are in pursuit, believing that God will give us that kind of breakthrough and ultimately release to us a "cancer free zone."

In spite of our many breakthroughs with others, I arrived at my own *Valley of Baca* when my dad died of cancer following a six-month battle. It was as though I pushed against a thousand-pound rock for six months; it never budged. Spiritual disease can set in when any of us has disappointment that is not brought into the open for God's healing touch. "*Hope deferred makes the heart sick...*" (Prov. 13:12). I knew that allowing disappointment to dominate my heart would cause a blinding of my eyes to the hand of God working in me.

Strengthening myself in the Lord helped me to stay away from anxiety long enough to make an important discovery: next to the thousand-pound rock is a five hundred-pound rock that I couldn't have moved before the battle for my dad's life. Pushing against the rock that never moved actually strengthened me by reinforcing my resolve to live in divine purpose and to establish the backbone of perseverance. By refusing to change my focus, I discovered that I can now move the five hundred-pound rock that I couldn't have moved before the battle. To keep myself from the sickness of heart warned about in Proverbs 13:12, I monitored the *attitude* of my heart. This was one way of turning my valley of weeping into springs of refreshing, for it is from the heart that all the issues of life flow. (See Proverbs 4:23.)

I can't afford to have thoughts in my head that aren't in God's. It's a great misconception to think that God gives cancer—He doesn't have it to give. I refuse to blame God for my dad's cancer, or any other calamity in life, for that matter. We simply live in a world of conflict and sin. Bad stuff happens. While I may not understand "why," I do understand that neither God nor His covenant is deficient.

While God is big enough to use every situation for His glory, it doesn't mean that the given problem was His will. Not everything that happens in life is God's will. We must stop blaming Him. The cornerstone of our theology is the fact that *God is always good and is the giver of only good gifts.* He is always faithful, and always keeps His promises. There is no evil or darkness in Him.

His goodness and faithfulness become the focus of my praise. I celebrate those aspects of His nature during what sometimes appear to be *contradictory circumstances.* After my dad's death, I discovered the privilege of giving God a sacrificial offering of praise that I will never be able to give Him in eternity. My offering was given in the midst of sadness, disappointment, and confusion—none of which will I ever experience in Heaven. Only in this life will we be able to give an offering with that kind of "fragrance."

If we fall short in our pursuit of a miracle, the lack is never on God's side of the equation. When the disciples were tempted to think in that way, Jesus gave them insight into the real issue, saying, "*This kind can come out by nothing but prayer and fasting*" (Mark 9:29). Most of us who fast and pray tend to do so in pursuit of a specific miracle instead of pursuing a miracle lifestyle. Jesus neither fasted nor prayed in this situation because His life was filled with prayer and fasting, which gave Him access to the desired supernatural way of living. We must think in terms of gaining access to a *lifestyle* instead of only obtaining a one-time breakthrough in a specific circumstance. We owe the world around us that kind of a heavenly demonstration.

Learning to face the possibility of lack on our end, without succumbing to guilt and shame, is key to maintaining focus in the pursuit of the Christ-like life of miracles. I refuse to sacrifice the revelation that *God is always good* on the altar of human reason because of my need to make sense of my seemingly unanswered prayer. I much prefer the discomfort caused by realizing an area of immaturity in my life if it will provoke me to pursue God until I get a breakthrough. Many who discover and admit to their need for personal growth in the midst of tragic loss fall into regret and self-criticism. Regret is a common killer in the church and must be dealt with—get it covered by the blood of Jesus and leave it there!

Use your loss as the foundation for another person's gain by calling for divine justice! That means I must continue pursuing the same breakthrough I was seeking for my dad, but now change my focus to others who have the same need. God's system of justice requires a thief to pay back seven times what he stole. I am asking God for a seven times greater anointing against cancer than I had before. (Interestingly, right after I wrote this part of the chapter, I received a testimony of another case of cancer healed through our ministry—*pancreatic cancer! That* is divine justice!)

You Have Been Summoned

An invitation is before us. We are living in days of revival in which God is bringing wonderful times of refreshing to His Church and drawing the lost to taste His salvation through mighty acts of power. But through this extravagant outpouring of grace, the Father is hoping to woo a generation of His sons and daughters to embrace the call to maturity, the call to contend in His strength for the personal breakthroughs we need to carry greater measures of His Kingdom power and love to the world around us. This is the race set before us. May we be those who learn to bring strength to ourselves, that we might run with perseverance!

Chapter 10

NOT ON MY SHIFT!

Through Him, we have authority over every storm.

Our call to disciple nations begins with the understanding of what it means to be a disciple. Jesus made the requirements to follow Him very clear: "*He who does not take his cross and follow after Me is not worthy of Me*" (Matt. 10:38). Jesus is not saying that we have to experience punishment for our sins. That alone was His cross to bear. Taking up your cross means embracing the truth that your life is not about you. Romans 14:7 puts it this way, "*For none of us lives to himself, and no one dies to himself.*" Jesus' cross was not about Him. His cross was about pleasing His Father and redeeming us. Likewise, our cross is not about us, but about living our lives for Christ and doing our part to make His mission succeed on earth.

The life of David shows us that personal breakthrough releases a corporate blessing to those around us. The Cross of Christ did the same thing, as it was Jesus' personal breakthrough. He had a destiny to fulfill that demanded great strength to be able to resist any temptation, distraction, or opposition that would turn Him from His course. His obedience released the greatest corporate blessing in history—salvation made available for the entire human race. Likewise, the cross we embrace will release a blessing, not only to the people around us who experience the benefits of Jesus' salvation, but to the Lord, who through our stewardship takes possession of His inheritance on earth.

Paul tells us that we are "*...heirs of God and joint heirs with Christ, if indeed we suffer with Him, that we may also be glorified together*" (Rom. 8:17). Jesus suffered by resisting the very things He would overcome through His death and resurrection—the kingdom of darkness and its reign of sin and death over the human race. Likewise, the cross we take up and the suffering that we endure as believers is the resistance of the enemy forces that we have been delegated to displace from the land that we have inherited with Christ. Exercising the power and authority we've been given to take our territory from the enemy is what strengthens our character to stand in a place of influence in that territory to establish the Kingdom. We're not merely to bind the strongman, kick him out of the house, and take back what he has stolen from us. We're supposed to become Kingdom strongmen who can release the blessings of Heaven to fill the house.

This is what Jesus was trying to teach His disciples in Mark 4. He told them it was time to pack up their ministry on one side of the lake and cross over to the other side, a region where they had not yet heard the message of the Kingdom. On the way they encountered a storm that attempted to destroy them. Jesus calmed the storm with a word and they were able to complete their journey. When they reached the shore, a demon-possessed madman came out of the hills and started worshiping Jesus. When Jesus cast the demons out, they begged not to be sent away from that geographical location. This indicated that the demons possessing the man were in control of the principality over the region. He had been their strongman to legislate an atmosphere of chaos in the area, and the storm that tried to prevent Jesus and His disciples from entering the region was a manifestation of their power. But their power was insufficient to keep the man from worshiping Jesus (no number of demons can stop anyone from worshiping Jesus!) The man's worship brought him under the superior authority of the Kingdom, and the principality over the region was displaced.

This disturbance to the atmosphere was so violent that the people in the region became fearful and demanded that Jesus and His disciples leave. Yet Jesus wouldn't let His new convert follow Him away from his own town even though it was an extremely hostile environment for a young believer. Instead, He commissioned him to lead His evangelistic outreach to the region: "...*Go home to your friends, and tell them what great things the Lord has done for you, and how He has had compassion on you*" (Mark 5:19). Some time later when Jesus returned to the area, every person in every city showed up to hear Him. One man's encounter with Jesus shifted the perspective of an entire multitude from rejecting God to hungering for Him.

When Unbelief Gets an Answered Prayer

It's a marvelous story, but we often miss the implication of a certain moment. After Jesus calmed the storm, He turned to His disciples and said, "*Why are you so fearful? How is it that you have no faith?*" (Mark 4:40). To many of us, His response seems a little extreme. We think it's our job to ask God to fix our problems, and it is His job to answer. But Jesus was saying, "I just had to do the job that I've trained you to do."

Jesus told His disciples that it was better for Him to go away because then His Father could send the Holy Spirit to dwell within us. This means that in the storms of our lives, we're better off than the disciples, who merely had Jesus sleeping in the boat with them. We have His very Spirit dwelling inside us. If we follow His lead, we will always have authority over the storm. But when we try to save our lives rather than leaning into the assignment and destiny that the Father has given us, we are not only costing ourselves an opportunity for a personal breakthrough in our faith; we are costing the people in the sphere of influence to which God has called us the opportunity to experience the blessing that is released when our faith displaces an oppressive atmosphere with a heavenly one. So many Christians look at the storms in their lives and the corruption in the world and conclude that their job is just to try to hang on until they die or until the Rapture. But people of faith have a different perspective—they look into the storm and see the opportunity of a lifetime. Through Him, we have authority over every storm.

Through Him, we have authority over every storm.

Spiritual giants have the habit of rising up during history's darkest moments to meet the challenge. People like Jonathan Edwards, William Booth, John G. Lake, and Aimee Semple McPherson were true disciples of Christ who captured the understanding that everything Jesus did was a model for their personal assignment. They looked into the storms of their day—the manifestations of the kingdom of darkness in the territory they were convicted was the rightful inheritance of the Lord—and rose up with faith to displace those storms, declaring, "Not on my shift!" Knowing their assignment was to shape the course of world history, they refused to give in to the sheer volume of darkness that surrounded them. They saw that all of Heaven backed them in their *humanly impossible* assignment.

Now is the time to allow the stories of these men and women of God to do more than awe us. Jesus never intended that only a few special believers would walk in a great anointing like His to change the spiritual climate over regions. He had trained every one of His disciples in that boat to do what He did. It is time for a whole generation of believers to embrace the opportunity before them—to take up their cross and contend for the breakthroughs that will allow God to entrust them with measures of anointing great enough to take back the inheritance we are invited to share with Him.

To do this, we will need great courage because we will be required to take risks when we step out in faith into what we've seen and heard from the Lord. We will never take that step if our hope rests on experiencing another great event, like waiting for the next wave of revival to sweep in or a prophet to call us out and give us a word. We must take personal responsibility to strengthen every weak place and break our agreement with fear. We must become the ongoing manifestation of revival and stop waiting for outside circumstances to line up with our dreams. We do this by giving thanks and rejoicing, praying as He prays, meditating on promises and testimonies, and associating with people of faith—not just when others around us are doing so, but continuously, as a lifestyle.

Utilizing these tools is the only way we can access the strength and courage we need in the midst of the storm because they remind us of who we are and what God has commissioned us to do. Most of all, they remind us that we are fully equipped for victory, not because we have a formula that always works, but because *God is with us and within us.*

This is His promise for every son and daughter who hears the call to contend for their promised land:

> *Have I not commanded you? Be strong and of good courage; do not be afraid, nor be dismayed, for the LORD your God is with you wherever you go* (Joshua 1:9).

Author Contact Information and Ministry Resources

Bill Johnson

Bethel Church

933 College View Drive

Redding, CA 96003

Website: www.iBethel.org

www.BillJohnsonMinistries.com

Ministry Resources

How to Overcome Disappointment

2 CD Set

The Christian life is the life of short accounts that doesn't allow unresolved disappointment to fill the heart. When what God has said is abiding in the believer's heart, it prepares them to hear when God speaks a Divine invitation into the impossible.

By contending in weakness and disappointment God is proclaiming promises into our lives, unveiling our stewardship of past disappointments and qualifying what we will carry in the future.

www.BillJohnsonMinistries.com
www.iBethel.org

Mission Possible

1 CD Set

God gave us the impossible assignment to disciple nations. Within that command is the enablement to see it performed. Through examples of recent events of heavenly invasions, this teaching ignites the listener to the awareness of how close Heaven is. God opens this inheritance to the church to give understanding and access, to know what we already posses that which attracts the outpouring. Be stirred as you turn your heart to heaven, inviting His presence to come even more.

www.BillJohnsonMinistries.com
www.iBethel.org

REVOLUTION: ERASING THE LINES BETWEEN THE SECULAR AND THE SACRED

Single CD

When the believer comes into the Kingdom, there is no such thing as a secular part of their life; everything becomes purposeful. God is leveling the playing field of the Kingdom, where the businessman, school teacher, stay-at-home mom and wife—the "minister's of the Gospel"—live with significance to shape the course of worldwide history. By giving a complete "Yes" to God, they step into a role of living on the edge of what God is doing, making it the center of what is to come.

www.BillJohnsonMinistries.com
www.iBethel.org

HEALING: OUR NEGLECTED BIRTHRIGHT

6 CD Set

Any area of a person's life that is not under the influence of hope is under the influence of a lie, and hope is the atmosphere in which faith grows. It is natural for a Christian to hunger to see impossibilities bow at the name of Jesus because we are a people born to confront and reverse the works of the devil. This series is a practical tool to discover the full provision of the Cross and how Jesus has enabled us to be successful in fulfilling His mandate.

www.BillJohnsonMinistries.com
www.iBethel.org

THE ADVANCING KINGDOM: A PRACTICAL GUIDE TO THE NORMAL CHRISTIAN LIFE OF VICTORY AND PURPOSE

4 CD Set

The strategies of hell are to distract and derail us from God's agenda through accusations and intimidation. The safest place for the believer is not in defending what we have, but in positioning ourselves for advancement. It is the sacrificial lifestyle that creates an atmosphere around the believer that insulates us from the destructive tactics of the devil and enables us to walk in increasing victory and joy.

www.BillJohnsonMinistries.com
www.iBethel.org

Leading from the Heart

8 CD Set

God has raised up true leaders the same way for centuries—with training that begins with the heart. Skills can be learned, but a Christ-like heart comes through repentance, discipline, and encounters with God Himself. Our faithfulness in these areas determines how much authority we can be trusted with. This series addresses the multifaceted characteristics of a leader who walks in loyalty, grace, wisdom and most importantly, with a value above all for the Presence.

www.BillJohnsonMinistries.com
www.iBethel.org

THE QUEST: FOR THE FACE OF GOD

4 CD Set

Our initial response to God is our salvation, yet the "quest" lies within our ultimate response to seek and experience His face. He is the center. As we experience the Face of God, we discover a new identity outpouring of influence and favor that empowers us to change the course of history. Join the quest—it is all consuming and glorious beyond description.

www.BillJohnsonMinistries.com
www.iBethel.org

From Glory to Glory: Biblical Patterns for Sustaining Revival

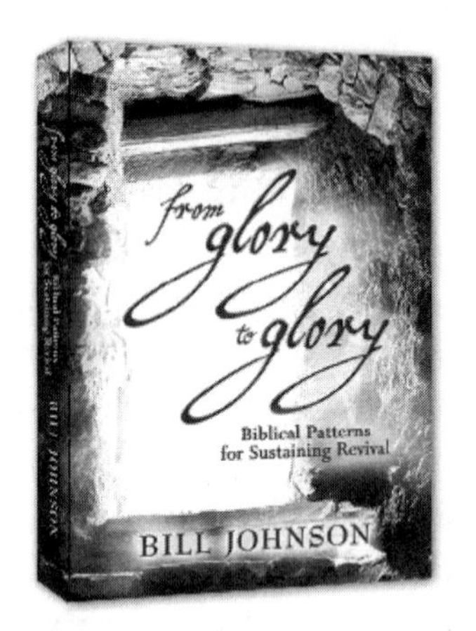

4 CD Set

Every believer has the responsibility to carry revival as if they are the only one responsible. God's manifest presence and favor marked the church of Acts with uncompromising standards which caused the message of the church to increase in its power and demonstration. This message illustrates how Kingdom increase is the calculated devotion to a move of God; exposing some of the tests that prove our readiness for more, and how we capture the favor and attention of Heaven through a lifestyle of faithfulness and honor.

www.BillJohnsonMinistries.com
www.iBethel.org